Best of the
Kudzu Telegraph

Best of the
Kudzu Telegraph

John Lane

Spartanburg • 2008

© 2008 John Lane

Editor: Jeremy L.C. Jones
Proofreaders: Thomas L. Johnson, Trina Jones, Margaret Ann Mabry, Michel Stone, Betsy Teter, Patrick Whitfill
Cover & kudzu photographs: Mark Olencki
Book design: Mark Olencki

First printing, September 2008
Manufactured at McNaughton & Gunn Inc., Saline, Michigan
Printed on paper containing 20 percent recycled content

Library of Congress Cataloging-in-Publication Data

Lane, John, 1954-
The Best of the Kudzu Telegraph / by John Lane.
p. cm.
A collection of essays from the author's Spartanburg Journal column.
ISBN 978-1-891885-60-0
1. Lane, John, 1954---Homes and haunts--South Carolina--Spartanburg. 2.
Country life--South Carolina--Spartanburg. 3. Natural history--South
Carolina--Spartanburg. 4. Outdoor life--United States. 5. Lane, John, 1954- 6.
Spartanburg (S.C.)--Biography. 7. Spartanburg (S.C.)--Description and travel.
8. Spartanburg (S.C.)--Environmental conditions. 9. Spartanburg (S.C.)--Social
life and customs. I. Spartanburg Journal and the Carolina Spartan. II. Title.
F279.S7L357 2008
304.209757'29--dc22
2008028932

Hub City Writers Project
Post Office Box 8421
Spartanburg, S.C. 29305
864.577.9349 • fax 864.577.0188
www.hubcity.org

Table of Contents

Foreword
Lyn Riddle

When Community Journals began publishing the *Spartanburg Journal* in 2005, we knew we needed a columnist whose voice was strong and clear. We got that—and more—in John Lane.

His "Kudzu Telegraph" has appeared in every issue of the *Journal* and from the start was a must-read for Spartanburg residents. His foundation is the environment, but the column is so much more. "Kudzu Telegraph" offers a mirror of our times, always with an eye on where we are headed.

At the root of most every one of John's columns is the question: what will be our legacy?

It is not easy to write a column, to have something important or revelatory or moving to say, especially every week. It is akin to standing naked in Madison Square Garden with 80,000 people, all with their own point of view, reading, criticizing, analyzing.

But John is fearless in his pursuit of making a point—and making a difference—in people's lives. He never forgets what unfortunately many in the news business these days have forgotten, and that's that he is writing for the reader, not the privileged, not the powerful, not the patrician.

John has taken on big business in columns about a mega-landfill proposed for Spartanburg County. He has raised the caution flag about unbridled growth. He has written about his travels, always with an eye on what Spartanburg can learn from other places.

And he has described with great compassion and clarity some of the more difficult experiences of his own life, such as a tribute he wrote to his mother-in-law when she passed away. He makes every word count. The telling details of a situation shine through in perfect prose.

In John's hands, the story always comes alive; readers share the moment with him. They learn and grow and pause for a moment at least to ask: what is our legacy? Where are we headed? Where have we been? What lessons should we have learned?

Just as John has his Monday morning ritual of walking his dog, getting a cup of coffee, and heading into his study to write the next "Kudzu Telegraph," I have mine. I check my inbox to see what this master poet has on his mind this week.

Lyn Riddle is editor of Community Journals, which publishes weekly newspapers in Spartanburg, Greenville, and Anderson.

The Kudzu Telegraph: A Brief History
Jeremy L. C. Jones

Every Monday morning since May of 2005, John Lane has risen with the sun and sat in front of his computer to write his weekly column, "Kudzu Telegraph," for the *Spartanburg Journal*. Often, Lane has a few notes scribbled on scrap paper, or he follows a compelling image bouncing around in his head. Sometimes, he comes to the keyboard with no plan, and other times he surprises himself with a drastic change of topic.

Writing on a weekly deadline is daunting enough. But writing a weekly column in a small city has its own complications. For one, you will run into readers who recognize you from your photograph and byline. And, if you're John Lane, a champion of the underdog who for years saw himself as the guy sitting behind the TV tray, throwing the mashed potatoes at the people on the screen, being recognized by your readers may not be the best thing to go with, say, a sandwich at the busy Café on Morgan Square.

Like his recent book, *Circling Home*, the columns in this book are acts of extreme courage. This may seem a little overstated, but … well, I don't think it is. You see, Lane writes about his neighbors, about the people who live within miles of his home. He writes about himself and about other people he must face each day, and he takes on a huge responsibility: to be compassionate, tell the (sometimes unpopular) truth, and live with the consequences of his publicly-expressed opinions.

I had the privilege of meeting Lane in 1999 at the South Carolina Book Festival in Columbia. He mentioned Spartanburg during a Q & A session, and I introduced myself, because at that point, I hadn't met many people who had even heard of Spartanburg (which is also my wife's hometown).

Early in our conversation, I mentioned some black-and-white

photographs I had seen hanging at the Sandwich Factory (now the Café at Morgan Square). "Hey Mark," Lane called across the crowded room. "You've got a fan!"

My first impression of Mark Olencki (who did the cover photograph and design for this book) was that he loved his camera. My second impression was that he and Lane looked an awful lot like twins—with beards, shaggy hair, and those delighted looks of constant discovery.

Over the following weeks, Lane sent me *Weed Time* and *Against Information*, two of his early books. He also sent a few of the first titles by the Hub City Writers Project, the esteemed Spartanburg literary organization that John co-founded and continues to serve. Finally, he forwarded me the proto-"Kudzu Telegraph," a digital newsletter (created and disseminated before the word "blog" had moved into the popular lexicon) full of that potato-throwing discourse mentioned above.

At the time I had no idea that I was meeting Lane at a pivotal point in his career—the point at which John Lane the Wandering Poet was becoming John Lane the Nature Writer. He spoke of doing more non-fiction writing, of doing more essays like the ones he had done for *Creative Loafing* and a number of other venues. As I remember it, he spoke of doing a trilogy of "place-based" books— which would later become *Waist Deep in Black Water*, *Chattooga: Descending into the Myth of Deliverance River*, and *Circling Home*, all since published by the University of Georgia Press.

What I did know for certain was that Lane was teaching me to love Spartanburg—*all of Spartanburg*, not just the green parts or the wooded parts or the waterways.

Come to think of it, it's about time someone comes right out and says it—John Lane *loves* Spartanburg. And he shares that love by telling the stories of Spartanburg in the "Kudzu Telegraph."

Lane's passion for his subject reveals itself in thrilling ways. He has an astounding ear for dialogue. So, of course, he often gives the best lines to other people. He has a sharp eye for the telling detail.

He picks just the right gesture, angle of light, or nuance.

Just when Lane seems to write best about animals—deer, tree frogs, butterflies—he captivates us with a river adventure. He writes with as much intensity about old maps or a favorite pickup truck as he does about the socio-political issues that concern him—land use, sustainability, and urban planning.

Lane focuses on the "ground under [his] feet," and with an emphasis on his own community comes a deep sense of responsibility. He does not write merely to meet a deadline. He is "most interested in speaking for the places that have become sanctuary through neglect, abandonment or abuse." In this way, Lane is an advocate, not a social critic.

Or, put differently, he doesn't call for change because he hates the status quo, but because he wants the best for this land we live on.

Overall, Lane forces us to look closely, to re-consider (or consider for the first time), and to think. He does this, in part, by layering his ideas in such a way that you can scan for content, re-read with growing satisfaction, or—as I have discovered on more than one occasion—you can go over them line-by-line with a class full of college students.

The forty-eight columns in this book are culled from roughly 120, published between mid-2005 and the end of 2007. They are arranged chronologically with one exception. The last piece, "Why Write about Nature?," was written in April 2007. I put it last because, in some ways, it speaks most directly to what Lane does and who he is. If you want a road map for reading these columns, start with "Why Write." Or you can save it for last and see if you agree with Lane's assessment of himself.

Well, maybe you shouldn't take my word for it. I am clearly biased. See for yourself. Read on!

Jeremy Jones is a freelance writer, editor, and part-time college professor living in Boiling Springs, South Carolina.

Snakes

Every spring I'm reminded that the world is bigger than us puny humans. I hear the big green voice of the planet in the trill, mysterious calls of tree frogs filling the woods when I open my study windows. I watch the gold finches work the newly-opened wildflowers in the meadow behind our house. I even see the immense, strange beauty of the creation in what crawls uninvited onto our porch.

My wife, Betsy, opened the front door last night and nearly stepped on a five-foot black rat snake. Betsy screamed bloody murder. She likes to hear me wax poetic about gold finches and tree frogs, but she draws the line at snakes.

"What's a snake good for?" my sister-in-law asked last week after a copperhead bit their big friendly Weimaraner on the face and front leg. The dog swelled up as big as Porky Pig, but survived. "I'd get rid of them all," she said. "Every last one of them."

I know there's danger—the rare bite of a poisonous copperhead in the Upcountry—but that's not enough for me to want to vote snakes off the planet. I think of what we've already eliminated from the Upstate out of fear, profit, or meanness—cougars, black bears, elk, the Carolina Parakeet, the woodland buffalo. I imagine all the habitat turned to subdivision since we arrived in the eighteenth century with our primary set of human needs, all the game trails paved and leading somewhere important to us—cities, towns, malls.

In spite of it all, snakes are still among us. They're survivors, a living link to wildness and deep time, though even the poets aren't often kind to them. Mary Oliver describes a water snake preferring "sweet black water and weeds" to her company, and James Dickey warns of snakes lurking in the kudzu, "striking under the leaf heads."

The biologist E.O. Wilson says one of our deepest instincts is what he calls "biophilia," a love of living things, and I count snakes among those creatures within my love circle.

"That's all fine," Betsy says. "But I still don't like 'em." Okay, I'll admit learning to love such stealth, danger, and clamminess is a long mile on the road to heaven, but some among us have learned to walk that mile. Fear of snakes is not a universal fear, though it often looks that way.

We have neighbors who tell us they cleared their whole yards out of fear of snakes, taking every last patch of undergrowth out and sowing a one-acre lawn with fescue. They can look out the windows and see the snakes coming across the mowed sward from a distance. I'm sure they drive by and look at our yard and call it "snaky," and maybe they're right. There's plenty of cover for animals in our snarl of grapevines, sapling dogwoods, and leaf mulch. A lawn doesn't fit our idea of home ownership. We prefer for our house to look like it grew naturally out of the surrounding woods. Betsy would just prefer a little more warning about what moves naturally through it.

I tell her one friend keeps a log in his truck of how many snakes he's seen dead or alive on Interstate 26 on his weekly drive to Charleston. His accounting is not exactly science. He's never done anything with the data. He just likes to keep up with snakes. I ask him if there are more or fewer snakes now than when he started almost twenty years ago. He says it's remarkably steady, year in and year out. They seem to be doing okay in South Carolina, at least in the territory I-26 bisects.

I've been keeping count myself. My own species count is now up to six in our Spartanburg eastside neighborhood—black rat snakes, black racers, a king snake, a copperhead, a northern water snake (Lawson's Fork Creek forms our back property line), and numerous tiny eight-inch northern brown snakes, one of which Betsy swears reared up in the woodpile and bared its fangs at her. I show her pictures of copperheads, try to bring her around to Wilson's "biophilia," tell her every step out the front door should be a journey into the wilderness, and she has to learn to be alert. She prefers for me to be Daniel Boone and sends me out to clear the path.

So I went out, picked up that black snake, and carried it like a visiting dignitary up the hill above the house. I released it into the leaf mulch and watched it glide away into our woods. As it disappeared I gave thanks that spring had arrived once again, embodied by the visitation of yet another serpent.

—May 27, 2005

A Snapping Turtle in
a Pickup Truck

"Snappers are the most widely distributed of North American turtles ... they are abnormally reclusive, and when one makes a public appearance it is not an event to be passed over lightly," writes my friend Franklin Burroughs, a Lowcountry South Carolinian transplanted thirty years ago to Maine.

Burroughs is writing about a big female snapper he'd chanced upon in the dirt road in front of his family's farmhouse in Bowdoinham. "They come out in late spring," he writes, "or early summer ... They need sandy soil to lay their eggs in."

It's mid-June in South Carolina, so I was not surprised at the bagel shop this morning when a man wearing a cap in a big white Ford 4x4 pulled up with a large snapper sitting quietly in the truck's bed. Taking Burroughs' advice, I was also not about to pass this event over lightly. It isn't every day a creature with a Southern pedigree dating back millions of years shows up in the strip mall parking lot.

A crowd gathered at the back of the pickup where the good-natured man had dropped the tailgate so everybody could see. The big muddy turtle sat calmly on a sample sheet of brick veneer in the black-ribbed bed liner.

The turtle in the pickup was about a foot and a half long, from nose to tail. This was a mature adult, but I knew from field guides that they could grow as heavy as thirty-five pounds with a shell the size of a manhole cover. It was, as Burroughs points out about the one he'd seen, out of proportion—its head too big, and body too small. It looked as if it had been stuffed into an armored breastplate that was too small for it.

Snapping turtles are like teenaged boys gone bad—all people seem to remember about them is their foul tempers and ruined reputations. Their jaws are rumored to snap broomsticks, and legend says they don't let go until it thunders. So goes the reputation. This captive one in the pickup seemed more contemplative than that. Betsy pointed out its hooked upper jaw and the holes of its nose, and she said the creature looked almost human. It looked a little like Yoda in the latest *Star Wars* to me.

Children nuzzled up for a closer look. Their mothers eased them even closer, a science lesson right here at the bagel shop. It was the closest thing to a living dinosaur they'd ever see.

"Where did you get it?" someone asked.

The man explained how he'd stopped out in the county and picked it up crossing a state road. "Just grabbed it by the tail and heaved it in," he explained.

"Do you do this often?" someone else asked.

"I stopped once and picked up one so big I flipped it over on its back in the front floorboard of the Sidekick. Had to tell my wife it was dead to get it home."

I observed that the turtle was most likely a female, probably crossing the road in search of a sandy patch to lay eggs. "You know the roads really take a toll on them."

"She's cleaned out," the man said. "Look how muddy her tail is now."

"Are you gonna eat it?" Betsy asked.

"Grandpa probably will," the man said, and the fate of the turtle became clear. She would end up protein in a big pot of "cooter stew" before long, an indigenous Piedmont food stretching back thousands of years. I'm sure the Cherokee had turtle stew in June, when the snappers crawled out of what Burroughs calls "the boggy, miry waters they inhabit." Snappers are such voracious eaters—fish, frogs, snakes, small mammals, ducklings, even dead things—it's hard to fault our neighbors for turning the tables on such a successful predator. Raw duckling for one and turtle stew for the other, on up the food chain.

Though I'm all for keeping alive the native food-ways of the Piedmont, of which bagel-eating is not one, I worry a little about these wild creatures still being prized meat in the county. Not everyone who picks them up would think about whether they have laid their eggs or not. And most people would not even slow down if one were lumbering around two or four lanes of traffic. Most often they're killed crossing roads, and I've heard this has devastating effects on their populations.

So, soon as the excitement passed, the man in the white pickup slammed the tailgate shut and Saturday morning business went on as usual on the Eastside. He drove off with his turtle meat on the hoof for Grandpa, and we went home to the suburbs, watching the roadsides for traveling snappers.

—June 17, 2005

Old Field Succession

When I weed the wildflower garden I'm attempting to grow over the septic field in our backyard, I always get frustrated and ask, "Why are there so many maple saplings I have to pull up?" I don't want maples. I want wildflowers. Well, the opportunistic maple seeds will keep sprouting up as long as they can compete for the nutrients and sunlight they need to grow.

So why, a friend asks as we drive around Spartanburg's sprawling Eastside, are there so many "big box" stores suddenly springing up? "Maybe it's the same thing," I say. "Opportunity. It's a capitalist form of old field succession."

"Old field succession?" my friend asks. "I thought we were talking Wal-Marts and sprawl, not college biology."

"We are," I say. "In a metaphoric sense."

"Oh, I forgot," he says. "You're an English professor."

"Well," I continue. "Big box stores moving into an area is not actual succession, but it's sort of like it. Real succession is an ecological process in which plant communities replace one another in a cleared or disturbed area until equilibrium is finally reached."

"Equilibrium," my friend says. "Now that sounds good. Can there be equilibrium among big box stores?"

"Well, in natural succession it takes a long time. In the first year of succession, a spot of bare ground, an old farm field or an abandoned building site will be covered with crabgrass and horseweed."

"Sounds like my front lawn."

"Well, leave your lawn alone and a year from now the asters will move in and the broom sedge, then three or four years down the line you'll naturally get some pines and you won't even have to buy them at Lowe's garden center."

"I'd like that."

"Finally, much later you'll get hardwoods, just like the ones they probably cut down to build your subdivision."

"Old field succession, huh."

"Yep, species emerge, have their time in the sun, and then disappear from the scene as other species become dominant."

"But what if I don't like what's dominant?"

"You can't stop succession in an old field. The only way to alter it is to weed out the new stage, retarding the succession."

"So, if you like wildflowers," my friend says, getting the idea, "you'd better keep pulling up those little maple saplings."

"Correct. "

"So what if I don't like all these dominant big box stores shading out all other locally-owned businesses in my community?"

"Well, big boxes are hard to pull up."

"Yep, hard to get your hands around them."

"Maybe they're a natural development in the 'ecology' of a community. They sure seem to prosper."

"Ecology of a community? Aren't you mixing your metaphors here?"

"Well, scientists might argue I'm stretching things, but ecology is the science of relationships in the natural world, and like it or not, a Wal-Mart is still part of the natural world."

"But what about regulations and ordinances—laws that limit big box stores coming into a community?'

"Well, that's like buying a big bottle of Roundup. It's one way of controlling things."

"But if a Wal-Mart is a plant, is it kudzu or an oak tree?"

"Well, Wal-Mart is a native species, so it can't be kudzu. Wal-Mart's homegrown right over in Arkansas, but it seems to flourish anywhere there's cash."

"So what would you suggest? How do we grow the kind of commerce we want in a community?"

"If we don't want multiple Home Depots and Wal-Marts and such we've got to stop buying stuff."

"Buying stuff?"

"Yep, consumption. That's their sunlight, their nutrients."

"You mean we've got to buy less?"

"Yep, all of us, including me. That's the only way corporations will stop opening big box stores— if their profits decrease. There are more big box stores because 'we' (as in the citizens of Spartanburg County) spend lots of money at them."

"Oh, I get it—maples grow toward the light."

"And multinational corporations seek profit and colonize *any* area where they can find it."

"Look around."

"We have seen the enemy."

"And it is us."

—July 8, 2005

The Real Southern
Connector

A few weeks ago I paddled with several friends from just below Pacolet to Lockhart, on the Pacolet and Broad Rivers. It was a distance of twenty-five miles. When we put in above Grindal Shoals, the Pacolet River was clay-colored and bold after a wet week of June showers. Our two canoes made quick time.

We floated five hours on the Pacolet through a world of river birches, blue sky, and heron flights. We didn't see a single house from the time we put in until we took out at our campsite just past the Pacolet's confluence with the Broad. It could have been the eighteenth century down there on the Union/Cherokee County line except for two road crossings and an occasional Styrofoam cooler floating past.

As I drifted on the river I thought about how Union County is an outdoor paradise. They've got everything I love down there— low population, open land, wildlife, and free-flowing rivers like the Pacolet, Broad, Tyger, and Fairforest Creek. Yet many in rural Union County dream of creating lakes and building interstate highways to remake paradise in the image of Greenville and Spartanburg to the north. In a world where tourism is the biggest growth industry, Union's got the goose and the golden eggs. It has space, history, and quiet—things that are quickly fading in the Upcountry as urbanization creeps south from Charlotte and north from Atlanta.

Some down there hope farm fields, pastures, pine trees, and hardwood groves will become an industrial corridor and "save" their rural county from double digit unemployment. But "progress" hasn't solved unemployment in Spartanburg, the urban county where I live. When I got home from canoeing I did the math—Union County's ten percent unemployment means they have 1,300 good people out of work. That's not good. Greenville County has a "low" unemployment rate of 4.9 percent, but that means they have over 10,000 unemployed, more people out of work than any other county in South Carolina.

And what about Spartanburg, the home of BMW and the interstate "Crossroads of the New South?" There are four times as many unemployed people in Spartanburg County than there are in Union and Cherokee counties combined. Yet Union seems determined to pursue development projects that will alter the rural nature of the county in pursuit of dreams that have proven fleeting in the Upcountry.

Paddling along, I thought about how sad it will be if twenty years in the future a four-lane "Southern Connector" cuts through the deep rural county south of Spartanburg and "opens up" that country to the mess we call progress. "This river," I thought, "is the real Southern Connector."

Give me a free-flowing river any day over an industrial corridor. Industrial recruitment is not going to fill our dreams anymore. The invisible hand of Adam Smith has passed over the Piedmont twice (first the iron industry, then textiles) and is now writing the industrial history of the planet in China and other points north, south, east, and west. If we want to invest in a $250 million "connector" in a future industrial corridor we should probably look at putting our dollars between Shanghai and Peking, not in the rural Piedmont.

Floating through wild, isolated Union County I thought how we in the Upcountry need to reinvent ourselves, just like the Yankees in New England did in 1880 when we stole their mills. We're not going to do it with four-lane highways or $8-an-hour jobs distributing Mickey Mouse figurines.

We need real vision. We need to recover our pride in what brought the Industrial Revolution to the Piedmont in the first place—our landscape and a remarkable array of free-flowing rivers falling out of the mountains only forty miles west.

I'm leaving tomorrow with Betsy for our summer vacation. We're flying to Wisconsin to drive around that rural state for a week. We'll paddle their rivers, stay in small-town lodging and eat local foods. We're not looking for man-made lakes big enough for jet skis or four-lane highways to get us quickly into country that's been "opened up" by dreams of industrial progress. It's river towns like Pacolet we're seeking, and we don't want to arrive there on an interstate.

We'll leave some money behind as good tourists always do. In the next twenty or thirty years I'd bank on there being a lot of people like us within a hundred miles of Spartanburg, searching for a place like Union County—some rural destination offering a quiet river trip, a hunting weekend, or a drive on a highway that's not clogged with truckers trying to cut twenty minutes off a trip from I-26 to I-85.

I hope there are people on the Union County Council who have experienced the Pacolet, as I have, from a canoe seat and realize these dreams of damming rivers and carving up paradise have nothing to do with real progress.

—July 22, 2005

Cans and Boxes and Catalogues

It's Sunday morning, and in an hour or so I'll load the pickup for the recycling run. We live in the county, so we don't have a blue curbside container tended by city sanitation workers on a regular weekly schedule. It's up to us. We make the decision—throw it away and watch it disappear from our lives in a black plastic garbage bag, or keep it around for a week until one of us remembers to haul it off. It's do-it-yourself out here in the land of libertarians, low taxes, and freedom from civic services like sewer and garbage.

I'll pull up to the containers on Fernwood-Glendale Road and sort through our three bins from the "recycling center" we've set up in the mudroom—one for glass, plastic, and aluminum; another for newspapers and the reams of catalogues, exhausted magazines, and scrap paper we accumulate each week; the last for cereal and snack boxes, a virtual mountain when the boys are home, a molehill when it's just the two of us.

I like the people I see there as well. It's hard to predict who will show up with a trunk full of bottles, cans, and papers, but by their bumper stickers I will know them. There are Kerry Democrats, Right-to-Lifers, and "W in 2005" Republicans. All types recycle, so there's hope.

Recycling is something we've actually learned to look forward to, even though at first it was a little too much like my mom saying "'clean up your room" when I was a kid. I've learned to like the ritual—glass here, paper there, cardboard flattened and slipped through the slot—and I've also learned to like the idea that every load of recyclables we take to the county's bins is one more load that that does not end up adding a few inches in altitude to some regional landfill, some trash mountain in someone's backyard.

My weekly recycling run is my personal revolution against conspicuous consumption. Every cereal box that's not hauled to the poor end of some South Carolina county and buried at a handsome profit by Waste Management or Republic is one more pine tree not processed into cardboard, one more useless item pressed back into community service by the people, for the people.

It occurs to me as I drive to the recycling center each week that waste and its management is a little like the tobacco industry thirty years ago—a very profitable industry based on people's laziness and addiction. The addiction is to convenience, to paying someone else for easy solutions to difficult problems. How do we rid our houses of our household trash? How do we disappear all the garbage that comes out of our county each week? We pay someone to do it for us—whether through private fees or taxes. We fill our trash cans with whatever it is we do not want and bargain with an industry to haul it away. We don't care where it goes. It's gone. It's not our management problem anymore.

It was worse in the past. In the not-so-distant decades most people out in the county took their garbage and threw it in the nearest gully. Some people out in my neck of the woods still believe that's the solution to garbage collection: find a low place and fill it up. You can see the black bags of trash tossed off bridges, the old sofas hauled to remote roads and abandoned in the piney woods.

In the early 1960s city garbage was not hidden in black plastic bags but was collected, can by can, in dump trucks, and hauled, load by load, to city dumps. Then it was deposited there and "recycled" by the poor before being burned. My uncle remembers building a whole bicycle from parts found at the city dump. One neighbor knew the exact spot where the out-of-date candy was purged each week from the local five-and-dime; once the kids found out the Hershey bars and Milky Ways arrived on Tuesday they couldn't resist. It takes a long time for a candy bar to go bad. It seemed worth the risk.

Not working on recycling as a primary value is a bad management practice, but I understand why the big corporations don't encourage it. It's for a similar reason the oil companies want new energy sources brought on line slowly. They like our laziness.

The next time you hear a politician tell us we have a looming trash problem and we need to let some big corporation come into a rural area and slap a 1,000-acre regional landfill next door to our neighbors, just remind them how dismal our local recycling rate is—nine percent, the lowest rate among metropolitan counties in South Carolina.

Tell them recycling's a good thing and really pretty easy to do. I'm headed out right now with my cans and boxes and catalogues. Let's meet down at the recycling center.

—August 12, 2005

Good Vine Gone Bad

August brings on the Dog Days, crickets in the grass, and poplar leaves turning yellow. It also means the local kudzu is in bloom. That's right, the kudzu's in bloom. Get out this week and see for yourself. Walk to the edge of any huge green expanse of the vines in the county and look up. High in the trees you'll see the flowering vines everywhere. Look on the ground and you'll likely see the little flowers of this naturalized import from Japan spread at your feet. It's enough to make you want to write haiku.

Right now I've got a vase filled with spikes of fuchsia kudzu blooms on my desk. The room smells like grape jelly. I've also been looking at the tiny blossoms of this member of the pea family, moving the parts of the bloom the size of a penny from side to side with the tip of my pen. I've identified the parts of the flower—standards, sepals, wings, and keel. At the center of each blossom is a tiny yellow blotch that helps guide in the bees, butterflies and hummingbirds, the local pollinators. The patch is the color of the sun on a little kid's first-grade painting. Pick up a flower off the ground and see for yourself.

I find the long complex story of this immigrant from far away instructive. Kudzu hasn't always been the villainous vine everyone loves to hate. It too was once among the admired new plants with a great horticulture future, uprooted and shipped to a faraway land.

Kudzu came to this country in 1876 as decoration for a Japanese garden at the Colonial Exposition in Philadelphia. The plant's lovely blooms made it a hit. The purple fragrant flower caught the attention of East Coast gardeners, and for sixty years it was a popular vine on arbors and trellises. Maybe it was mostly planted as an annual up in the cooler North where it wouldn't "winter over," but it never really got out of hand. Back then I imagine it was a great deal like wisteria—beautiful where it was contained and always fragrant and lovely when it bloomed.

By the 1920s farmers had discovered kudzu wasn't merely beautiful; it was also tasty to livestock and could provide forage, so they planted for that purpose as well. Then, in the 1930s, kudzu took on the job we usually associate it with—large-scale erosion control in the South. The Soil Conservation Corps employed it as their organic tool of choice for stabilizing acres and acres of railroad embankments and eroded gullies. In the late 1930s the SCC planted 85 million kudzu seedlings along new highways all over the United States. The Corps also introduced two other "exotics" as erosion control that still plague our Southern backyards—multiflora rose and Japanese honeysuckle.

By 1953 the feds had realized the vine with the green card was actually an aggressive invader ready to occupy the South from within, so they discontinued the practice of subsidized planting. I'm not sure if anyone has planted a vine on purpose since.

So decade by decade, kudzu's positive character was lost to history, and now we're left with a vine no one has anything good to say about. Other Japanese imports have settled in better. Some have even become common in Southern gardens—bamboo, honoki cypress, flowering plum, and Japanese maple. But not kudzu. No one has to plant it for forage anymore. Cows turn up their noses. Only the goats seem to like it. It's made the Roundup stockholders a fortune.

In spite of its bad press, there are still those out there trying to broker a truce with kudzu. There are local food lovers who make purple jelly from its blossoms and folk artists who twist the woody vines of the hardy plant into baskets. Others who have not bought into the free-trade coffee movement brew tea from its blossoms, and those who have an eye for environmental art look at the small sheds and old cars and bushes it has overtaken and see a rich topiary landscape all around us. Who needs a bronze statue of Daniel Morgan when we've got kudzu forming shapes in all the county's empty fields?

Don't get me wrong: I preach kudzu removal as much as the next Southerner. After all, it does cover more acres than Sherman burned on his march to the sea. It's time to get serious lest someone call me a kudzu hugger. Yes, I've seen the kudzu flower and smelled its wafting fragrance, but I still get out my clippers and cut all the vines I can find out of trees. I fight back. Just because this invader from the East had a clean start in a Philadelphia garden over a century ago doesn't mean I should ignore the fact that it long ago went bad in the heat below the Mason-Dixon Line.

—August 19, 2005

Deer in the Headlights

There was a dead deer on East Main Street early one Sunday morning.

We saw it as we drove to breakfast. It had stiffened up, laid out among the crepe myrtles in front of Hollywood Video.

When I brought up what we'd just seen at the bagel shop, a girl in the booth behind us said she'd spotted a deer running through the Publix parking lot at Hillcrest Shopping Center a few days earlier.

I concluded, with only circumstantial evidence, that it could have been the same deer in a happier moment. What had brought it out of the woods and into the growing asphalt jungle of Spartanburg's upper Eastside? It was a puzzle worth pondering over coffee.

When we passed again an hour later the deer had reached Eastside celebrity status. There was a young woman photographing the white tail corpse with her cell phone.

By the end of the day on Monday I'd heard at least ten people comment on the dead deer. It's not that a road-kill deer is a rarity in the South Carolina Upcountry, but this one caught everybody's attention in the middle of the sprawl, so close to the Hillcrest Shopping Center. After all, there shouldn't be much to interest a deer along densely developed East Main.

"Maybe it was returning *Bambi* or *The Yearling*," one student joked when I told him about the surprise road kill I'd seen. "Maybe it was late fees."

The wild and the tame are increasingly mixed up these days. Driving to school yesterday I saw ten wild turkeys in a neighbor's Eastside suburban backyard. They seemed quite content grazing in the fescue.

Once a year, usually about this time, a wandering bear will somehow sneak across Interstate 85 and end up in the backyards of some Spartanburg suburb on our side of town.

In *The Beast in the Garden*, a recent book about the return of cougars to Boulder, Colorado, David Baron reports that many species—bears, raccoons, foxes, beavers, deer and turkey—are reclaiming old territory.

Because of the larger numbers of wild animals and larger numbers of people, it's harder to draw the boundary lines.

"The presence of almost 300 million people," he says, "inevitably transforms, alters, and distorts the natural world in myriad ways."

In the last decade, Baron says, there has been a coyote in downtown Seattle, another captured in Boston, and in 1999 one was caught in New York's Central Park.

"Lands being developed and neighboring lands being restored …Today's American frontier is an increasingly fractal edge that, like a craggy coastline, enhances the area of contact between … the urban and the wild."

The contact on East Main between this deer and somebody's bumper caused a little stir in me when I saw it. First, I felt sorry for the deer—sorry that it had wandered so far from cover; and then, of course, I worried about its unsuspecting driver. Dodging a deer is not what would be on most of our minds after passing Hardee's, the LongHorn Steakhouse, and an overpopulation of drug stores.

I'm not a hunter. If the deer had been killed from a tree stand I would have felt differently, but as far as I could see there were no tree stands in the Hollywood Video parking lot. Deer have evolved in close relationship with predators, so hunting seems a more fitting way for one to head for the Happy Hunting Ground than crossing East Main Street.

Hunting helps control South Carolina's overly-healthy deer population. There are more than 170,000 licensed hunters in South Carolina, and this time of year they go into the countryside and kill 300,000 of the estimated 900,000 deer in the state. Let them have at it.

Hunting gets people into the woods to commune with nature and out of the commercial districts like Hillcrest. Hunting even puts meat in a bunch of freezers and gets cooks out of the Publix parking lot for a meal or two. It's become a necessary piece of the puzzle we call conservation. I'd rather have deer controlled by hunters than by Toyotas, Buicks, and BMWs.

I hope the city removed that deer from the Hollywood Video lawn. I hope the coyotes and the vultures are dining on the carcass of that unlucky beast somewhere under the stars out in the county.

And I hope it's the last dead deer that we see on East Main this year. I'd rather complain about the Eastside looking more like the Westside every day without the complications of wildlife management to think about.

—October 14, 2005

The Carp Man

Once, several years ago, a friend of mine took me to visit the Carp Man of Lake Hartwell. I'd be willing to bet New York doesn't have a Carp Man. I'm not even sure they've got carp.

When I arrived at the lake, I walked out on the Carp Man's dock, and he came out of his sailboat. I could already see the Carp Man's huge mysterious school of carp roiling in the water around the slip. Fins and bubbles danced on the surface of the lake all around the dock. The Carp Man greeted me warmly, then opened his plywood chest and handed me three loaves of stale bread.

"How many are there?" I asked. The mysterious carp were gathering in the water below where I stood. They already knew it was feeding time.

"Maybe a thousand," the Carp Man said. "You can try and count if you want."

"And they're always here?"

"You just get out the bread and they'll come up. They're just like goldfish. But don't get me wrong. They're still wild animals. One time somebody tried to pick one up, and all the others disappeared for a week. Ever feed a wild fish? Just do it like this." The Carp Man folded a piece of stale white bread in half and held it about an inch out of the water. "They might be wild, but they don't have teeth. I wouldn't let you do something that dangerous."

The wild carp rolled and smacked at the bread, and the soggy wheat slices disappeared down the round gullets of the huge carp.

I held the bread tentatively over the water and pulled back each time they smacked at it, finally tossing the piece of white bread in the rolling mass. The Carp Man laughed.

"Sometimes they'll swallow your whole finger, but you can just pull it out. Remember, they don't have any teeth."

Okay, I thought. This is about experience. This is about learning. This is about vision quest and spiritual growth. So finally I let the carp eat from my hand, and the Carp Man was right. They ate the bread and my finger came out clean as a whistle from the round sucking mouth.

The Carp Man is retired military, a former combat glider pilot from World War II. "Some people call me the Captain," he said. "But most call me the Carp Man."

He's been feeding that snarl of carp for over a decade and says some of the fish have a personality. "That one over there is always one of the first up here," he pointed to a big carp with a scar on his back. "Sometimes even turtles come," he said, "and I feed them too. The carp bat them around like volleyballs." He laughed.

Then the Carp Man threw a stale honey bun in the water and I watched it disappear in a wave of fins and mouths. "They like that, too: bread, hot dog buns, honey buns, anything I can get at the grocery stores for my carp. I feed them dog food sometimes, too." He brought out a plastic cup, slung dog food pellets over the water, and that disappeared too, the carp rushing to the surface.

When the children came, the Carp Man seemed happiest. "I always supply the bread the first time, but if they come back I expect them to bring their own. And they can come back any time they like."

The Carp Man said once or twice people have fallen in. "There was a drunk woman once who fell forward. You know how light your head gets leaning down? Well, she came down after a party to feed the carp, and keeled right over. But it wasn't very hard to get her back up on the dock. She was so afraid those carp would eat her that she floated back up soon as she hit the water."

—January 13, 2006

Paddle to the Sea

Mid-winter is the time for outdoor adventure dreams.

Since we moved into our Eastside Spartanburg house and I first saw Lawson's Fork flowing through our backyard, I've dreamed of getting in my canoe and paddling to the coast.

It's an urge I get every time I look out the window and see the ceaseless current passing by. Rivers all go somewhere, and I know ours ends up in the Santee delta, 200 miles east, twenty miles down the coast from Georgetown. I want to follow it there.

Interstate 26 shadows the old river system all the way from the Upcountry and I've driven it a million times. On that highway we can get to Charleston in three hours. It probably takes the current I see out my window about two weeks after passing our house to flow down Lawson's Fork to the Pacolet and then on to the Broad, the Congaree, through Lake Marion (which before becoming the Santee-Cooper lake system was the Santee River) and on down the old Santee to the Atlantic.

Last summer I talked five friends into dreaming, too. "Paddle to the Sea," I started calling it. The plan was to take ten days and float to the distant Carolina coast over spring break in early April of 2006. Cooler heads soon prevailed, as Frank Burroughs, one of my floating companions, took a string and actually traced the "river miles" from here to the sea and calculated a trip of 270 miles. "I can paddle twenty seven miles a day," he said, "but I don't want to do it for ten days in a row." It wouldn't be impossible, but with all that could go wrong—bad weather, low water, fatigue—we decided to only go from here to Columbia on the first leg, a comfortable distance half that long. Planning the expedition this way, we'd leave a little something on our adventure plate, and tackle the Columbia-to-the-coast leg another season.

Long-range river voyaging is a type of time travel. Floating the Santee system from the Upcountry to the coast was quite common in the eighteenth and even nineteenth centuries. Why not use gravity to get to Charleston or Georgetown? Back then the roads were bad and river pace was once hardwired into our souls. Everybody who reads *Huckleberry Finn* longs to kick back and float a river. "Low bridge/Everybody down/Low bridge 'cause we're coming to a town," I remember singing in elementary school. "Fifteen weeks on the Eerie Canal." Does anyone sing that song anymore?

First the railroads killed river travel, and now the interstates are the new rivers, hauling freight from town to town, the old rivers flowing under them like ghosts at a hundred bridge crossings.

Ours will not be the first "Paddle to the Sea" from Spartanburg. I've heard that the late Sam Manning, local legend and former legislator, paddled alone in the 1940s from here to the coast as a little vacation before being shipped overseas. In January of 1969 Wofford's athletic trainer Dwane "Doc" Stober took seventeen students down the river from Pacolet to Charleston. Finally, in June of 1999 David Taylor, a former Converse professor, floated from Glendale to Columbia in a blue kayak and wrote an account of the trip in the first (and only) issue of *The Upcountry Review*. I'm sure there have been other trips, but these are the only ones I've heard about.

Steve Patton is one of the friends who will float with me in April. Steve has also paddled to the coast from Spartanburg. He took the trip in late April and early May of 1981. He was alone in a wood canoe that he and his dad had built by hand a few years before, and he says he now looks forward to repeating the route—this time with company.

Last weekend as a little warm-up, Steve and I drove south into Newberry County and put Steve's current canoe, a less romantic plastic Coleman, on Parr Reservoir, a South Carolina Electric and Gas lake built in 1944 shortly after Sam Manning would have passed downriver on his voyage.

Parr backs up the Broad River for seven miles. Steve wanted to paddle a few miles from a boat ramp down to the twenty-five-foot dam and see if there's a decent portage route to get us back into the river channel below.

On a cool foggy January day we paddled into a stiff headwind two miles down to Parr Dam. We hauled our canoe out on a grassy bank at the dam's south end and saw the Broad River flowing out of the lake through a spillway into its ancient channel.

Steve was relieved to see there is a clear portage through the woods back to the river. I was happy to be sitting on the grass bank of a river with low clouds racing above us. As we ate lunch I imagined being back in that spot in eight weeks, three long floating days from home, lost deep in "river time."

—February 3, 2006

Born to Be Wild

Last week I took five of my Environmental Literature students on a hike around Wofford College, looking for wildness. It was a sort of voluntary "lab" for a course composed primarily of reading and writing, a way of getting out in the world and testing some of the concepts we were exploring in nature books and essays.

We'd read Emerson's famous essay "Nature," and Thoreau's essay "Walking," pieces I'd referenced as "founding documents" for those who write and read environmental literature today. Where in Spartanburg could we find Ralph Waldo's "original relationship with the universe"? I'd asked. "Where here around us might Thoreau's 'wildness' be 'the preservation of the world?'"

We considered these questions as we "sauntered," to use Thoreau's word, and circled the urban campus for a brief hour. Thoreau is known to have walked for four hours a day in the New England woods, but surely, adjusted for a century and a half's inflation, an hour's walk might do.

Emerson's "original relationship," the students agreed, would be no problem. After all, Waldo had found his crossing the Concord commons surrounded by mud puddles at midnight. We could probably find ours at Wofford. But Thoreau's wildness might be a more thorny issue. I reminded them we weren't looking for wilderness—which we would surely have no luck finding in the middle of Spartanburg. We were looking for wildness instead.

"How about down at fraternity row," one joked. "We could start there." I reminded him this was literature, not sociology.

So where might we look, and for what? In class the day before, the students had speculated that what Thoreau meant by "wildness" in the 1840s was some sort of lack of human control. "What's free," one said. "That's clearly what's wild—no control outside itself."

That was pretty good, and so we started glancing around looking for some person, place, or thing that might fit.

Soon we stopped at a big tulip poplar tree on the front campus and talked a little about what Thoreau might consider wild. I pointed out how this was a large specimen of a native tree, with seeming security in its surroundings. Its gray trunk is probably five feet around. Was this eighty-year-old tulip poplar wild?

The students looked around. There were maintenance workers fertilizing the lawns, the sidewalks had been neatly edged, and the fallen leaves had all been removed. Not much wild here except maybe this native tree.

Nearby was a quite large southern magnolia in front of Old Main. It surely looked wild, but it's not native to this region. Does that matter? Is there wildness in the massive magnolia? Does it share in Thoreau's "preservation of the earth?" I wondered out loud, "Does that freedom you talked about in class fit either the poplar or the magnolia?"

Wofford's campus is a designated arboretum. I joked that I'd heard someone wanted to implant significant trees on the campus with computer chips that would activate and announce the tree's name. "Tulip poplar," I intoned like a mad horticulturalist. The chip might contain other interesting information about the trees or the arboretum or Wofford as a strolling visitor with an iPod passed. Would this add or detract from the "wildness" of the place?

Some of my favorite books ponder these sorts of questions— Gary Snyder's *The Practice of the Wild*, Jack Turner's *The Abstract*

Wild, and Stephanie Mills' *In Service of the Wild* come to mind. Some of my favorite stories and poems place the issue of wildness clearly at the center of the narrative—*Adventures of Huckleberry Finn*, *Deliverance*, and *A River Runs through It,* for example.

"Is this one of Wofford's wild spots?" someone asked as we later stood on the slope of a landscaped gulley and listened to water falling over stones from an artificial water feature called the J.R. Gross Cascading Steps along a passage of the Liberty Trail between Wofford and the Regional Medical Center.

These students were perceptive. I do feel more in touch with wildness there. There is something about that spot that fits the script for wildness more than anything on the ridge-top "classical" campus, established in 1854. Maybe it is the water, the way current flowing over stones always makes for freedom. In spite of the landscaping, the mulch, the non-native cultivars placed on the Liberty Trail, the running water returns some wildness to the spot.

So we finished out our walk and ended up back among the buildings and clipped lawns of Wofford's front campus. Did we find wildness as we sauntered *a la* Henry David for an hour? Did we approach what Thoreau in "Walking" calls "the Holy Land?" We glimpsed it, I'm sure.

As we walked the campus the students became more interested in the idea of wildness and began to see this familiar landscape around us as a place where some might be leaking through. Isn't that what a good education is all about?

—February 24, 2006

Another March Madness

In a few weeks we will be able to officially say, "spring has sprung," but last week, on one of the warmest nights of winter, the chorus frogs cranked up strong and loud. The whole floodplain behind our house sounded like a tiny army was hidden in the brush, all running their thumbs down the length of their plastic combs at the same time—"creeeeek, creeeeek, creeeeek." The squeaky song went on all night with unceasing devotion to the rhythm, a call and response chorus, a one-note, bug-eyed symphony.

Of course it was a natural love song we were hearing with the windows open for the first time. Tiny platoons of amorous frogs (an inch or so long, the size of a big button) were courting in the grassy swales and moist woodlands. We've got plenty of that watery terrain, and the resident frogs take clear advantage of it.

Also called "swamp tree frogs," the chorus frogs call from shallow isolated puddles of water left over from the last time the creek left its banks or after a cold winter deluge. These puddles serve as temporary love nests for these seasonal swingers—no Las Vegas Hilton or Niagara Falls hideaway, but they fill the purpose. The frogs prefer these watery wastes we call "bottoms" for their yearly courting, singing all day and night if the temperature's right.

After the singing stops and summer creeps in, they're hard to locate. What seemed an army just melts back into the creekside landscape, not to be heard or seen again until next spring. It's more than a one-night stand, but not much more.

Scientists say populations of amphibians are diminishing world-wide as we build more roads and houses, clear more riverside forests for agriculture, and their old habitats shrink in size and quality. The ozone depletion and the weather changes have their effects as well, but one reason we built our house where we did was so we could hear this yearly shout-out for love while it lasts. At the first sound of vernal frog-longing we throw open our windows and the house fills with it. The song gives us hope that maybe we can actually find a way to co-exist, for species to do their courting in each other's presence.

Our singing next-door neighbors drop me into my own March Madness. For a month or so frogs become my obsession. I listen to recorded frog songs in the truck so I can sort out the species that are cranking up around us. From year to year I forget some of the songs and always need a refresher course for this amphibian jukebox.

After rains I watch the black top with care so as to not silence any of the frogs crossing the low-lying roads around the large floodplain of Lawson's Fork. I drive slowly and pick my way among the leaping frogs bent on courtship. I even bought a mobile of green tree frogs (of which the chorus frogs are a tiny cousin) for our bedroom, and we watch as they spin in the breeze from the open window. It seems strange to hang frog effigies when there are so many outside. But that's one thing art does: remind us of our connections to everything around us.

Of course the frog sounds have made me start looking around for other signs of spring, the season of universal courtship, of earthly renewal. "The song of the world becoming," that's what poet Pattiann Rogers calls it. I've noted that the first horns of green have appeared on the blackberry cane; the twirling vines of yellow jasmine are now following the sun's climbing path with new runners; the iris is pushing out of the warming duff; and the tiny sheaths on the buds of the cottonwoods have unhitched and fallen on the trail.

It's not just the plants that are beginning to respond. Other animals can tell the seasonal change is underway. On the deck, a familiar tribe of anoles has started sunning regularly on the south-facing railing, and I'm watching the abandoned phoebe nest on the front porch light fixture to see if she returns to raise a brood.

But mostly it's the frogs that reset my time clock for spring. Soon the spring peepers will also join in, and if you try real hard you can sort the strands of sound and pick out the congregations of cricket frogs, green frogs, pickerel frogs, and leopard frogs. By April it always sounds like a wholesale frog party with no adult supervision.

Let them go at it in peace. The world's a big place. It's bigger than our need for ignorance or control. It moves along a path much wetter and wider than the route to work and back. It's so easy to forget we're part of a cross-species world community so much bigger than the human family. That's why this time of year I listen to what's going on in the watery wastes.

Right now a cool rain is falling. More is expected tomorrow. Open the windows in your bedroom tonight and listen. See if you can hear the sound of spring approaching. It will be the frogs calling each to each.

—March 10, 2006

The Not-So-Constant Gardner

"A lawn," says writer Michael Pollan, "is nature under totalitarian rule." We opted for a wooded lot, and so I like to think of our place as always in a state of natural anarchy, more hippie commune than Soviet empire. We planted no grass. We left all the maturing hardwoods and the undergrowth in place. What grows here is what grows—sweet gum, red oak, river birch, red maple, and lots of the twisted trunks of sourwood.

Even the infrastructure of hospitality is laid back. There is a short meandering mulch trail to our front door rather than an arrow-straight paved walk. We have to put out a lantern when we have folks over so they know to walk down our trail and not the driveway.

The cleared spaces near the house are covered in clay-colored Broad River gravel and have a vaguely Asian theme. When we plant in the stone-lined raised beds it's mostly with native plants. There's a stone swale sweeping around the house for drainage, and it looks like a dry creek bed. Near the front door there's a wild-looking bog we have filled with pitcher plants and even a Venus flytrap. I get great pleasure out of finding insects in the house and feeding them to our carnivorous bog.

"Your yard's so natural," a friend said when she visited. "It's like living in a tree house."

This style of free-form gardening is not without its problems. It's hard to keep the Broad River gravel clean of vegetation. Stretches of it fill up every spring with volunteer weeds, and we have to clear it or we'll have the lawn we didn't want. Betsy prefers Roundup, but I like to jerk it all out by hand.

We still have to water, especially with the inconsistent weather of the last several years. Of course we opted not to install an in-ground sprinkler system. Our front yard's holding its own, though. With a little work it looks the way we want it to—"woodsy," that's how Betsy describes it as we gaze out toward the street from the front windows.

It's the wildflower meadow in the backyard that's been the real battlefront, the place where my laissez-faire attitudes about gardening have run up against the plant politics of low maintenance.

I call what's quickly filling the wildflower meadow behind our house "fall asters," but Betsy calls them "weeds" and wants them out. She's watched how in three years this particular species of aggressive native plant has displaced the expensive "native Southern mix" of wildflowers we've ordered online in hopes of charging the empty space above our septic field with seasonal color. These asters have invaded like Huns. They want our whole backyard, and they want it now.

It would have been so much easier to seed the open tract of red clay left from construction with grass, simply plant once, then mow it every week. But we wanted color, so we planted, hoped, and dreamed of something that would look like a mountain meadow out of *The Sound of Music*. We both have to admit it increasingly looks like a vacant lot.

It's sneaky the way the asters have taken over our flower show. The first year the wildflower meadow was filled with lovely red and yellow poppies, an annual supplement we broadcast for quick color.

The second year the perennials in the purchased mix took over, and in the spring and early summer there was a modest cover of black-eyed Susans, coreopsis, and a dozen others species. Underneath, though, the fall asters were already putting down roots, massing in the shadows of our planted perennials, gathering strength. By late summer spreading green clans of asters were muscling out the smaller plants. They were like storm troopers, taking over the yard foot by foot.

I tried to accept their invasion. I even considered letting them have the meadow, seeing their blooms as beautiful, but before the asters went to seed I pulled up as many as I could by hand. I tried to stop the invasion.

Now it's spring again and I look out at our wildflower space ready to be filled with color. I sit on our screened porch and plot to overthrow the kingdom of the asters. I've ordered a blend from our seed company called the "aggressive amendment." I tell Betsy if anything can compete with those asters it's an army of store-bought seeds with such a powerful name.

Maybe what we want—that natural look, low maintenance, and the freedom from lawn care—is a utopian dream, but I'm not ready to give up. Mostly we like the way our yard looks, even with the pushy asters. I assure Betsy that the weeds will be kept at bay. She's hopeful, but says she'll wait and see.

—March 17, 2006

Take Me to the River

On Friday when you're reading this, I'll be twenty miles down the Pacolet River, starting Day Two of a five-day float trip to Columbia. They're calling for good paddling weather—partly cloudy skies and temperatures in the 70s. Right now it looks like we'll have four canoes in our Upcountry flotilla. I know it sounds like the beginning of a bad joke, but along with me will be three college professors (one retired) and a lawyer. Filling out the bow and stern seats are three students, sons of one of the professors and the lawyer, ranging in age from ten to twenty.

We've heard the *Deliverance* jokes, which always surface any time you put a boat in a moving stream. "The *Deliverance* Syndrome," they call it. I try to be amused. I teach James Dickey's novel every spring and know how much damage his story has done to the psyches of some shy Southern suburbanites who can't think much beyond what Roundup controls along the trimmed edges of their yards. I tell those who ask we're worried about low water and sore muscles but not men in floppy hats appearing from the deep woods.

There is some danger out there, though. Turkey season opens on Saturday, and our floating interests will be competing with hunting parties along the shore. Each day when we're on the water we'll probably wear orange vests so that we're not mistaken for a game bird trying to escape by canoe.

Our gear will be distributed between each boat—tents, food, clothes, sleeping bags. Each canoe will be like a little moveable Budget Inn. It's quite a good feeling to know that for five days everything you need is along for the ride. The fleet is mortgage-free, and we carry no homeowners' insurance on the contents. Nobody ever thinks about resale value with a canoe.

It's strange how many people I've told about our trip didn't even know you can get to Columbia from Spartanburg by water. It's as if we modern Americans mostly live now in a geography made shallow and sketchy by interstate travel, on-board navigation systems, and soundproofed cars. For many people, it's as if strip malls and lube shops and apartment complexes were more real than the original world around us.

So, some may ask, why paddle one hundred miles to Columbia over spring break? Isn't Myrtle Beach enough? Can't Hilton Head fill the bill? Doesn't Dollywood offer a vacation package deal hard to resist? How about that timeshare in Fort Lauderdale?

I can't speak for those who float with me, but I paddle because the feel of water moving under a boat relaxes me and helps me forget about time, something I find comforting. I paddle out of a need to experience places from their original surfaces. I like to get below the pavement, the farm fields, the parking lots, the lawns.

I paddle because I'm a self-propelled kind of guy, so I enjoy letting gravity do most of the work. Besides, every time I put a paddle stroke in the water I like to think I'm countering the single stroke of an outboard engine somewhere on the planet. It's a sort of karma I've been working on for decades now—self-propelled river karma. If I hunted I'd probably end up a bow hunter like Ed and Lewis in Dickey's river novel.

What else? On a not-so-personal level, our South Carolina river systems are some of our most important recreational assets and they're under-utilized. ICAR, the International Center for Automotive Research, gets the press as the business future of the

Upcountry, and it probably is. Charleston still draws the tourists. What about our rivers?

Planners are just beginning to realize that every mile of navigable free-flowing stream is a moving personal resort if you've got the right gear. The largest kayak manufacturer in the United States is over in Easley. When those engineers and professors start flocking into Greenville and Spartanburg, I'm betting they'll be surprised no one has as of yet filled our local rivers with canoes and kayaks.

We won't be pioneering this river route. In the nineteenth century the Broad and Pacolet formed a highway system as reliable and familiar as I-26. It's only with the advent of good roads in the twentieth century that the rivers took a back seat to pavement. I'm recovering a noble pioneer pastime—watching the river flow, heading downstream to the next town and the one beyond that.

I'll be calling in next week's column from somewhere downstream when I can get some phone service, so check in to see what the float from Lawson's Fork to the Pacolet and on down the Broad has in store for our group of modern "River Voyagers." Maybe you too can paddle to Columbia on some future spring break. Maybe you can use the details of our trip as a road map for adventure right in your own backyard.

—March 31, 2006

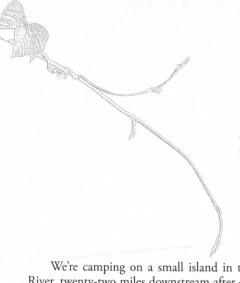

River Time

We're camping on a small island in the middle of the Broad River, twenty-two miles downstream after our launch last Thursday from behind my house in Spartanburg. It rained last night, and off the eastern tip of the island there's a rainbow, a good sign for the five days to come on the river.

There are six of us in three canoes on this small island. I sip my coffee and think about how we were supposed to camp on a friend's land downstream, but we were late setting up camp, and how could we turn down sleeping on an island? It was good enough for Huck and Jim in *Adventures of Huckleberry Finn* and so it should be good enough for us.

There's also a thin mist on the Broad, and two geese are making quite a racket over near the York County shore. The geese are watching me as I watch Frank and Ken stoking the fire for breakfast. Steve is just getting up, and both of Ken's boys are still asleep in the tent.

This is our second morning out. Lawson's Fork and Pacolet, full of fallen trees but beautiful in their small, intimate ways, are now behind us, smaller veins in this living circulatory system we call a river. Yesterday when we left Spartanburg, we miscalculated how much light we had, and it was deep dark by the time we reached our first campsite downstream from Pacolet Mills. As we floated in the dark, beavers slapped the water, and once a turkey flew overhead like a stealth missile headed for the other bank. The frogs formed a chorus in the low spots.

All day Friday we paddled down the Pacolet until we stopped at Skull Shoals to pick up the last of our crew, Ken's son Dunk, who had to attend class on Friday. His mother dropped him off with a re-supply, a homemade coffee cake we plan to eat this morning.

It could be the nineteenth century here and I could be Huck Finn if I were willing to ignore the nylon tents, the plastic and Kevlar canoes, and the aluminum pans Ken will cook with. The Broad was used for a few decades to move goods up and down from the coast. Less than three miles from where we're camped, an extensive canal system moved barges around the shoals at Lockhart. In the early mist I can almost see the boatmen poling their barges upstream.

It's easy to get caught in a fantasy like this on a river. When you're paddling a canoe it feels like time, as I've known it back home, loosens up—minutes, hours don't seem to hold as much sway. Instead, it's the length of the daylight and the way the light rises in the morning that matter most, that give the trip its borders. River Time, I call it.

Though we have only been here overnight, this sand bar has probably occupied this spot for centuries, a function of geology, hydrology, and weather. It changes from each flood, sometimes one way, and sometimes another. Sand has always been a symbol for time, and it's no different here, slipping slowly through my fingers as I sit and wait for breakfast. We're operating on River Time here, away from it all, and slowed down to river speed, a couple of miles per hour.

Not everybody's relaxed as we are. The rest of the world goes on with other occupations as we cook breakfast on our island. Turkey season opened this morning, and already we've heard the gobbling; every now and then somebody takes a shot from one of the two shores. Last night I thought for a moment there was an owl convention on the river until Frank and Ken, both occasional turkey hunters, pointed out that these were hunters imitating owls so the Toms would gobble and give up their roosting sites.

But enough talk about turkeys and turkey hunting. There's bacon frying over an open fire—and soon Ken will have another pot of coffee brewing. I tell Ken's son Grady to get up for breakfast, that I'm writing a column, and he might have to help me get out of it. He thinks for a moment and accepts the challenge.

"My English teacher says you can end any story with 'it truly was,' and add the title," Grady says, mixing up his first water bottle of Gatorade for the day. "You know, like 'It truly was … a heart of darkness.'" I think about the way the day is slipping past us. And so I give it a try: "It truly was … River Time."

—April 7, 2006

Spartanburg to Columbia by Canoe

How to put a week canoeing on an Upcountry river into perspective? Some of the numbers from last week's trip might help—six days of paddling, five nights of camping, 102 river miles, ten highway crossings, six dams portaged, a Heritage Preserve, two Revolutionary War battle sites, a Colonial canal, three old textile mill sites, two sites on the National Register of Historic Places (including an ancient Native American fish weir and an Indian mound), thirty canoe strokes a minute, six or seven hours a day, like a health club workout with moving water under it.

Long-distance canoe travel is like stepping out of time for a week. It's like turning in your membership to the Present, and punching your ticket for a life your great-grandparents would surely have understood.

The two pieces of technology necessary to get us from Spartanburg to the state capital were invented hundreds of years ago—canoe and paddle—but most of the desire to take such a trip was drained away long ago by fast highways and the time constraints of modern life. Six days to get to Columbia? Boy Scout troops might do it, but not grown men with access to automobiles and the interstate system.

But everyone is interested in hearing about such a trip once you do it. Since I returned, several people have asked questions: What about private property? Where did you camp? Did you see much wildlife? Did you meet many people on the river?

As far as private property goes, you're fine as long as you stay on the water in your canoe. Navigable rivers are our great commons, and for over half the trip to Columbia you're paddling through the Sumter National Forest, so a real sense of public ownership and wildness fills you as you look ashore.

There are plenty of private ownership clear-cuts along the way, and often it's obvious that the property owners really don't value their stake in the river valley. They often cut right to the water's edge, leaving only a tree or two as a buffer. Some education in forestry's "best management practices" would serve them well.

We camped on islands in the Broad three of the five nights—Goat Island, Henderson Island, and Haltiwanger Island. This string of islands in the Broad River is a state treasure and I wish they could be incorporated into some sort of long-distance canoe camping trail to make a trip like ours reasonable for more canoeists and kayakers. There are no posted signs on these islands and their official ownership is still a mystery to me.

And wildlife? We saw dozens of wood ducks and mallards and hawks, three mature bald eagles and four immature, herons, and cormorants nesting on a power pole in Parr Lake. Twice turkeys flew across the entire river in front of our canoes. We were often in consultation as to whether we had seen an otter. Most of the time these sightings turned out to be muskrats. Of course, deer are abundant, especially near the confluence of the Pacolet and the Broad, where we saw dozens along the shore.

And yes, there were even a few people along the way. Downstream at Lockhart, the power company provides a free shuttle around the dam. When we arrived and announced the presence of through-paddlers waiting for a shuttle, a power company employee pulled up in a comically small pickup to portage three canoes, six people and a mound of gear a half-mile around the dam. He sat in the truck and shook his head. He did his duty though and called in a company dump truck to haul us and our gear back to the river.

Once we passed two men fishing from canoes, and three others were fishing from kayaks, so we felt some kindred self-propelled spirit with them when we passed.

On Saturday we'd been out for three days and two nights. We were tired by the time we floated up to the boat ramp at Wood's Ferry, a campground in Sumter National Forest on the Chester County side of the Broad. We were waiting for our second wind.

There were three people fishing on the bank. One of them was a retired gentleman from some rural place nearby wearing a "Jesus is Lord" baseball cap. He watched as we landed the canoes and stepped ashore. He asked where we'd come from, as if a reasonable answer could have been "Mars." He'd seen plenty of bass boats come and go from the boat ramp but not many canoes. "Upstream," I said. "Spartanburg."

"This river comes from Spartanburg?" he said.

On Monday morning, our last day on the river, we paddled hard and made twenty-two miles before the Interstate 20 bridge came into view at lunch time. It was a shock seeing all those fast cars and trucks crossing the river in the distance, so much speed injected into our six-day world of four or five miles an hour. Less than a mile downstream a diversion dam channels all the water past Columbia into an old canal.

"That's interstate and we've been on the innerstate," Frank said from the stern as I looked up at the long-haul rigs passing.

We passed under the super highway and aimed for the Columbia Rowing Club dock. Out on the flat water behind the dam a powerboat put a local executive on his lunch break through his paces in a sleek white rowing shell. The interstate hummed above us. We landed. Our adventure was over.

Yes, Mr. "Jesus is Lord," this river comes from Spartanburg. And so did we.

—April 14, 2006

Yard Work

I still do what used to be called "yard work," manual labor, and so Easter Weekend I caught up on the demands of maintaining our little peaceable eco-kingdom.

We live in an oddly-shaped, sustainably-designed house on four acres of woods on the edge of Lawson's Fork's floodplain. Our house sits in what might be called an "ecotone," a place where the higher, dryer ridge meets the wetter floodplain below. The line is defined by changes in vegetation and temperature. This makes for lots of wildlife happy in each zone moving through our yard. It's as if we have a seat on nature's fifty-yard line for all the action all through the year.

There is no lawn in front or behind our house, but I've found other ways to spend as much time out in the yard as any proud suburban adherent to grass neat as a putting green.

I mulch our numerous river-rock-lined beds full of mostly native perennials and shrubs, weed the local clay-colored product called Broad River gravel that covers our walks and the areas most people would sod. Finally, out back, I mow what Betsy calls "the weeds," the volunteer fill-in vegetation in all the spots not taken up by woods, mulch, beds, wildflowers, or paths.

Mulch, you might say. How does mulch fit in? I used to hate

mulch and the way it makes a yard look neat and tidy, but I use it because it holds the moisture in the beds during these times of inconsistent rain. But make no mistake—we don't do multi-colored designer mulches here. Our color's one hundred percent natural.

All this yard work is quite a commitment, but it allows me time to ponder. I've found some of my best environmental thinking occurs while I'm doing yard work.

Sometimes I worry about things clearly human, like whether we remembered to mail in our taxes, but mostly as I'm working in the yard I think about connections—us, the house, the creek, all that's downstream. The natural world is like a spider's web. Was it John Muir who said, "Touch a strand and the whole web shakes"? I know everything I do to maintain our place in the woods has an impact on something else—the plants I choose, the gas mower I run, the methods I choose to keep the whole sprawling thicket beyond the edge of the house at bay.

Yesterday I spent an hour pulling up the Japanese honeysuckle creeping steadily into our wildflowers from the woods, now that spring is here. Honeysuckle is one of our resident "legal aliens" on the property, along with kudzu, multiflora rose, and others. As I bent low to pull up the honeysuckle by the handfuls, I thought with the extraction of each wiry clump how some governing body should have discussed the plant's future residence in my backyard before it became widespread. Sure it did some honest work as erosion control early on, but was it worth it?

Why not just take the easy way out and apply Roundup, the death agent of choice for most gardeners? Well, it's that web thing again. If I touch the honeysuckle with that herbicide then my backyard web will not only shake, it might just fall apart.

A recent University of Pittsburgh study has found that Roundup can be lethal to amphibians. I'm a believer in science and trust scientific studies, so I try to pay attention to what scientists are saying about the world long before the public finally accepts that something is wrong. It's like the canary in the coal mine. If

Pittsburgh reports I should be careful about my use of Roundup, then I try to be careful.

I like to see toads, frogs, and salamanders in our yard, and this is the time they're all over the place—particularly green and gray tree frogs, and toads of all descriptions. They seem content to hop around the yard. I'm content to see them.

And so I spend hours at the manual labor of pulling up the honeysuckle plants strand by strand, but the labor, manual or not, works for me. One sweep per week along the edge of the wildflower garden and I can keep the vines at bay. It's an organic choice, and it keeps our yard Roundup-free.

But where does it stop? What about my lawnmower and all these greenhouse gases I'm partially responsible for floating toward the sky? It's not possible to live, especially in the twenty-first century, without touching and, more than likely, smacking a strand or two on that web a few times as we move through our busy, labor-saving weeks.

So I'll just keep working outside and thinking. My time is not too valuable to spend on manual labor. It's actually one of the things that keeps me close enough to see my place in the web.

—April 21, 2006

Old Maps Tell Stories

The other night at Jazz on the Bridge, a yearly fund-raiser for the Spartanburg Area Conservancy (SPACE), someone started talking to me about old maps. He'd been to a flea market and bought one of Spartanburg County, had it framed, and hung it on the wall in the den. He said he likes to look at it and imagine the old places outlined on its surface. This got me thinking about old maps.

For centuries maps have been our way of making sense of the world, of finding things we've hidden, lost, or never visited before. They range from crude drawings on the backs of envelopes to be used once and tossed away after we find our destination to complex topographic maps in green and tan that one might need to walk cross-country or to lay out a subdivision. "To ask for a map," the writer Peter Turchi claims, "is to say, 'Tell me a story.'"

I've always been in love with the stories maps tell—how they can get you places, how they show you where you've been, and what the possibilities are for where you might go. I keep a folder under my desk with copies of every map I've been able to locate that covers the territory we call home: the lower Lawson's Fork in Spartanburg. I find the maps in libraries, in the files of rare book dealers, flea markets, anywhere old maps might go to live in the age of MapQuest.

In my folder are colorful old soil maps, geological maps that show deposits of minerals in the county, a railroad map from the late 1900s when Spartanburg was the "Hub City" of train travel, old school district maps, a 1954 farm map that records the names of farmers in the area, and real estate maps from the 1970s when all the subdivisions in town were new and the roads were freshly named.

It seems I spend most of my time pouring over copies of the five oldest maps I've collected, ones from the eighteenth and nineteenth centuries, including a crudely-drawn map a scholar friend found in the South Caroliniana Library in Columbia that could be from as early as 1770; the famous Mouzon map of 1775, showing "Roads and Indian Paths, as well as Boundary and Provincial Lines"; the Benton Map from 1791 showing the location of Revolutionary War battles in the county; the Mills' Atlas map of 1825, and the E.H. McCollough map of Spartanburg County of 1887.

Each of these maps has its own set of topographical charms. The crude map from 1770 looks like an early draft of a survey. It shows our rivers headed east, terminating as the heads of arrows. There are three or four crudely-sketched cabins along the way. The site of the upper shoals at Glendale is marked as a "forge." The only path or road is a simple trail of dots from the Enoree to the Broad River. The map looks like an old treasure map with photocopied water stains to give the whole surface an ancient cast.

Mouzon's 1775 map is much more elegant, with beautiful calligraphy. It sets off "the Catawba Nation (144,000 acres)" in a square to our east, and there is a boundary line from the Catawba River to the Reedy River, outlining Cherokee Territory to the west and south. The roads, still old Indian paths, look substantial, and it's easy to see them morphing into modern highways as the land passes from Native American to Colonial control. It's also easy to see how it's mostly in the creeks and rivers where the Indian names of things will survive.

The Benton Map of 1791 is interesting in that it shows a complex web of paths and roads converging on the area that is now Glendale. In the late eighteenth century, the place where SPACE holds its annual party was an important crossing point and "mill seat" with grist, sawmill, and early ironworks nearby.

The most famous of the early maps, and maybe the one my acquaintance found a copy of at the flea market, is the Mills' Atlas Map of 1825. This map was made for the first atlas of South Carolina and shows an expanding network of highways, many of which we would recognize today. "Spartanburgh" (with the "h" we lost sometime in the nineteenth century) appears as a crosshatch of settlement near the map's center.

McCollough's Map of 1887 finally peoples the territory. It's a postal map, and many of the old names we associate with the county can be found on it—Poole, Bagwell, Anderson, Chapman, Foster, Zimmerman, Cleveland, Moore.

Fine reproductions of several of these early maps can be bought from the Spartanburg County Historical Association. As you would guess, these old maps wouldn't help get you to Charlotte or Greenwood, but if you own them they can take you on a journey you can only imagine. I pull the old maps out all the time and pour over their surfaces, hoping to discover something I didn't know about our home territory—like White's Mill off Main Street was once called "McKee's Mill," or that the road to Pacolet we now call "U.S. 176" was once "Tolleson's Road to the Line."

I understand that all the new cars will soon have navigation systems that will actually talk you efficiently through to your destination—"Go left in 1.2 miles" and "Turn around and go back," as if travel is only about getting some place by the most direct route.

Paper maps will soon be as ancient and useless-looking as buggy whips or typewriters. It makes me sad to think of all that neglected territory out there that future generations won't travel by pouring over maps. What stories old maps can still tell, if we'll just listen.

—May 12, 2006

Eating in the Foodshed

The Hub City Farmers' Market opened on Saturday, and hundreds of people turned out downtown for the launch. Farmers' markets are nothing new in Spartanburg. This is the third location I've known since I was a boy. I remember going to the Kennedy Street market to what I've always called "the old farmers' market" with Mama to buy homegrown tomatoes decades ago, and the last few years there was one held in the parking lot near Morgan Square.

But hopes are high for this new manifestation of the age-old Southern tradition. Flip through Phil Racine's Hub City Writers Project book, *Seeing Spartanburg,* if you want to know what the "farmers' market" used to look like in Morgan Square on a Monday, the traditional "sales day." One of the most famous photos of the Hub City shows wagons, pulled by mules, filling the square in front of the Daniel Morgan statue on a Monday in the late 1880s. Farmers and traders came from all over the region to gather on the square for market day. They used the chance to catch up on gossip and do some shopping themselves.

Last Saturday, with the backing of the Spartanburg Nutrition Council and the support of the city, the summer air was filled with bluegrass music, and two rows of multicolored tents were set up on the green lawn in front of the Magnolia Street Station. Parking extended far back behind the depot in an area reclaimed from the kudzu. People came with high hopes and broad smiles. Now, once a week from early summer until fall, everyone in town will know where to purchase the fruits of local soil.

"Eating in the foodshed," that's what people nationwide call this movement back toward eating locally. The term "foodshed" is a play on "watershed," and it takes its power from that comparison. Watershed is a term for how water from smaller streams flows into a larger river. Foodshed describes the way food flows from areas where it's grown into the places where it's consumed.

So simply saying "foodshed" creates a way of thinking about local, sustainable food systems. Accordingly, eating apples from near Hendersonville or peaches brought from Inman and bought at the farmers' market is "eating in the foodshed." Buying that avocado with the little sticker on it from California, as good as it tastes, and eating it in a salad, is not.

Think for a moment about where most of your food comes from. I mean, think about every little bit of it—the coffee in my cup this morning is an organically grown Mexican French Roast, and the grains in my favorite cereal were probably grown somewhere in the Midwest. Both these items are tasty, but they are from a long way out of my foodshed. So far I haven't eliminated them from my diet, but being aware of where these foods originate changes my attitude toward them. Someday I might decide to find a cereal made from grains right here in my foodshed. The coffee poses a little bigger problem!

Food now "flows" into Spartanburg from everywhere in the world, thanks to the wonders of modern shipping. Purchasing avocados or Mexican organic coffee are two of these wonders of our contemporary lives. Another wonder is how cheap food from everywhere can now be. What is often not considered in the cheap "world food" equation, though, are all the hidden environmental, social, and human health costs of eating from world markets.

This weekend gas is $2.60 a gallon. Gas costs also figure into "eating in the foodshed." If gas tops $4 a gallon will it be worth it to truck exotic food into a place when much of what we eat could be grown locally?

Trying to "eat in the foodshed" helps us account for some of these costs if we want to, though even local food is not that simple now. Who truly grows these "local" foods? Is it the farmer selling them from the back of his truck, or does that farmer hire illegal workers to till, plant, and harvest these crops?

There wasn't much local food at the farmers' market on the first Saturday to ask these questions about. Those who came early got to purchase most of the fruit from our local fields. Because of this, the opening of the market was mostly ceremonial, though an hour into it a truck pulled up full of cantaloupes and watermelons, and the masses descended on it like something out of *The Grapes of Wrath*. Money was exchanged, and a few local shoppers walked away with a "foodshed" melon.

Under the colorful tents there were a few local crafts for sale, and some had brought flowers and breads and cookies. There was even a tent where you could buy organic dog cookies for twenty-five cents each. As a special treat I even let my dog "eat in the foodshed" for several mornings.

I hope the farmers' market becomes the central location to prompt Spartanburg to eat more in our foodshed. That would make it worth the trip to the train station for "market day." We don't plan to abandon BI-LO, but we do plan on strolling back through the market to see what turns up for sale.

—June 30, 2006

Country Foxes and City Foxes

A friend of mine wrote this week from her farm near Athens, Georgia, to say she'd had an encounter with a pair of grey foxes. It wasn't her first encounter with grey foxes on her property: "I see one maybe every other year, usually if it takes shelter in the tack room from winter rains." She said that she knew the foxes denned up at a neighbor's house across the creek and through the woods.

The afternoon she wrote, she'd been inside the pasture gate, giving the donkeys "some pre-dinner old bananas for treats," and then along strolled the pair of foxes less than ten feet from her.

She surmised it was the female in the lead, "because the male had to stop every three feet and mark territory." She watched as they strolled on into a big hedge and disappeared.

But the foxes were not gone after all. "By the time I finished feeding the animals and was back at the gate, the neighbor's dog across the street began to bark, so I just stood there. One of them came trotting briskly back the way it had come. It stopped to look at me and then retreated another fifteen feet before it turned, I guess to see if its mate was coming along. Then it slipped into the woods and headed for home."

I tell this story because my friend's country foxes in Georgia were joined this week in my imagination by two other grey fox stories, both recent encounters within Spartanburg's city limits. Several weeks ago, two friends stopped me at the farmers' market to tell me they'd seen a fox the night before on their back steps, right in Converse Heights. It was eating cat food from their pet's bowl. "Red or grey?" I asked. They weren't sure, and so I explained how we have two different kinds of foxes in the Upcountry, and how they are quite different in their habits.

Usually, I explained, when we say "fox" we think of the red fox, the common one fox hunters prefer to chase, but when I described the size and coloration of the grey fox—smaller, darker, more cat like, shyer than the red—my friends were sure what they'd seen was a grey fox. "A fox eating cat food, right near downtown," they said, marveling at their good luck.

Then when I told the story of the city fox in Converse Heights to another friend, he said he'd recently been walking his dogs along the trails in Duncan Park at night. In the woods he heard a sound he hadn't heard in his neighborhood before. "Like a crane in distress," is how he described it. He walked further along the trail, following the sound, and he came across a fox hiding under a fallen log, holding still while he shined his flashlight its way. "It must have been a young fox, a grey fox," Gerald said. "The dogs just stood there looking at it, and then we walked back home and left it alone."

Country foxes, we tend to believe, are common. City foxes, our good sense tells us, are out of place somehow. We like to draw hard lines between the wild and the tame, the raw and the cooked. But it's not really so. The lines are much thinner than we think.

It could someday get worse if we keep filling the Piedmont successional fields and woods with unplanned subdivisions. A few months ago another friend brought me an article explaining how foxes began to enter urban London from the countryside after World War II. It was easier to make a living there. Now foxes have spread all through suburban London. Some estimates place the fox population as high as sixteen foxes for every square mile of the city. In late winter, they say, in the London suburbs you can often hear the vixens (female foxes) with their eerie screams. Some say the sound is like a person in distress.

Do a little searching and it's easy to come up with stories about how, in this country, Denver already has a healthy population of red foxes living comfortably downtown, and you probably heard or about the coyote caught in Central Park a few months back. If there are coyotes in New York, surely foxes are in our neighborhoods, too. Who knows, maybe the only bobcats in Charlotte aren't in the basketball arena.

But our local grey foxes are much more solitary than those urban red foxes, and they probably like the woods more than the suburbs. "A wonderful mouser, rarely invades poultry yards; probably wholly beneficial," one field guide says of grey foxes. Grey foxes climb, unlike their distant red cousins. Cat food in Converse Heights will do if available, but they prefer wild fruit like grapes, blackberries, persimmons, and even pawpaws.

So I've been thinking this week about how people living in Duncan Park or Converse Heights might feel to know foxes are prowling their neighborhoods so close to downtown. I don't think most would approve. It's not that they can't be troublesome—occasional rabies, digging up flowerbeds, and of course eating all that expensive cat food.

But I still like knowing they're around. "The suburban wilds," that's what one writer calls the territory where most of us live in the early twenty-first century. Pay attention. Big tomcats aren't the only mammals ranging free through our Spartanburg backyards.

—July 14, 2006

Snakes in the Yard

It's been over a year since I wrote about snakes, but I think it's time. *Snakes on a Plane* has brought my reptile friends into the spotlight, and once again they're getting a bad rap.

I have enjoyed encounters with snakes for three decades now and still mark my years by the first snake I see in the spring. In the year 2006 it was a northern brown snake out in the yard, a slug-, earthworm-, and insect-eater only ten inches long. It turned up in some wood I was moving. I picked it up, admired it, and then placed it back under the log.

In 2005 my first snake sighting was more dramatic. On a warm day in March we were driving down Starline Drive and slowed to watch a young copperhead crossing the road. The snake had recently shed and was brightly patterned. I commented on how beautiful it was with its new skin, but Betsy reminded me the neighbors might not think so.

I grew to admire snakes in college. Though an English major and no scientist, I worked first at identifying snakes, and then understanding their ways a little better. I read Roger Conant's *A Field Guide to Reptiles and Amphibians of Eastern and Central North America* like a sacred text. I studied the range maps in the back. I kept live snakes as pets in aquariums, and I stopped to identify dead ones on the road. When I visited museums, I zipped past the monkey house and headed straight for the reptiles.

"So what was it exactly about snakes?" I'm sure you're asking right now if you are one of the majority of readers who fear them intensely. Well, I've reflected a great deal about that, and what I've come up with is this: It was peer pressure. I learned to admire snakes because a close friend did. Once I got to know them, snakes offered a door for me into the natural world I'd been waiting to open.

Snakes are good teachers. They offer us a way of understanding the ancient workings of a landscape, something I began getting interested in during college. As a class among the vertebrates (backboned animals), these creatures have a history millions and millions of years longer than our own. They've crawled onward through eons, adapted to conditions and survived in spite of asteroids, volcanoes, and suburbs. What is there not to admire and learn from?

And learning about them helped me quickly to put a few snake myths to rest as well. Snakes are not slimy; they are to be respected, but they are not aggressive, though they will try to escape when cornered; there are no poisonous water snakes in the upper Piedmont of South Carolina in spite of all those stories about unlucky water skiers falling into "nests" of "moccasins." If you don't believe this last one, just get a field guide and look at the range map for cottonmouths and notice how it ends in Columbia!

Back in college on late spring nights, rather than party, I'd ride with my biologist friend David Scott up on Highway 11 at sundown looking for snakes crossing the road. We had this wild idea back then that we'd get photographs of every sort of snake in the Southeast. After a year I gave it up and sold my camera. David is still at it. For twenty years he's worked as a research ecologist at the Savannah River Ecology Lab and his photos of reptiles and amphibians appear in books and magazines all over the world.

During our time cruising for snakes we saw a great many. Some were dead, unidentifiable splats of scales hit by speeding trucks and cars, but many were alive. I remember we saw black rat snakes, milk snakes, corn snakes, black racers, copperheads. We saw snakes of every color and length available to this landscape. It was better than a museum because there weren't any little signs telling you what you were seeing. You had to figure it out yourself.

If we saw a snake we'd stop, catch it, and haul it back to Wofford in a pillowcase to photograph in the courtyard of the dorm. David went to great trouble to get shots of snakes in natural settings, and he preferred to take his photos early in the morning when the air was cool and the snakes were lethargic and easy to pose. He'd twist them around a branch and they'd stay for a moment.

When we finished we'd slip them back into the pillowcase and take them into the dorm (breaking all the housing rules) until the next time we headed up the highway to let our quarry go near where they were caught.

I remember one night we saw a timber rattlesnake that had been hit by the car in front of us. We picked up the corpse, skinned it on the roadside, and brought back the skin with rattles attached. We kept that skin in our dorm room like a prize.

I'll have to admit *Snakes on a Plane* is a pretty good premise for a film—take at least two of people's greatest fears (flying and snakes) and put them together—but I'm not planning on seeing it. I'm happy with the private film always running in my head—*Snakes in the Yard*. It's always showing in a landscape near me.

—August 25, 2006

Fall Grapes and
the Poor Man's Banana

This week we've been practicing our wild food-gathering skills on our evening walk. It's an August ritual. All along the road we've started seeing muscadines, or "fall grapes" as the locals call them, ripe and ready for eating.

The Vikings named North America "Vineland," and it's easy to see why if you stop for a moment and look up into the edge of any wooded vacant lot or Piedmont forest parcel. You can trace the dark brown, papery shafts of the vines up from the soil along the trunks into the canopy as they push up for light. Above your head you can make out the distinctive scalloped edges of the bright green muscadine vine leaves snarled among the limbs and foliage of maples, poplars, and oaks.

An easier way to spot a vertical muscadine patch is to look at the asphalt as you walk along. This time of year you'll see the grapes in the ditches and on the shoulders of roads. Sometimes if the trees hang out over the road, they'll be scattered all the way to the center line. Most will be mashed by passing cars or people, but if you look closely you'll see enough ripe grapes to catch your interest and whet your appetite for wild fruit.

I'll admit it takes an eye for habitat and a lot of gathering to get a handful of purple-skinned muscadines. It's lots easier to go to

BI-LO or the Fresh Market and buy a plastic bag of green seedless grapes, but there's something wild and free about picking up a snack off the ground, biting a hole in the grape's tough skin, sucking out the sweet pulp and spitting out the tiny black seeds.

It's not the kind of fruit you'd want to sprinkle in when you mix up the chicken salad, or put in your kid's lunch sack, but the flavor of a muscadine is worth the trouble. It's a local snack food you're sharing with the raccoons, possums, foxes, and yellow jackets.

This time of year when we leave the pavement and swing down by the creek, the wild-fruit gathering gets even more exotic and exciting. There's a wild pawpaw patch along Lawson's Fork. The trees enjoy the moisture of the floodplain and their presence casts an almost tropic feel to walking through the streamside forest.

Pawpaws are small trees, often not much more than a shrub, really, never more than thirty or forty feet tall. Their trunks are slender and silvery gray, and the wood has no commercial value for timber. A pawpaw looks a little like a droopy, loose-jointed magnolia. Sometimes they are so abundant they form a thicket. Other times they stand in twos and threes among the box elder and privet. Standing among them with their foot-long leaves drooping in the dappled sunlight of the streamside, you'd swear you were in Brazil or Costa Rica.

It's the pawpaw fruit we love. In spring we watch the small dark flowers appear on the twigs and know soon the tasty fruit will follow. All summer we watch the dull green, oblong berries grow bigger above, often two hanging side by side. By August they've grown into the shape of a small, green gourd and attained the length of a thumb. We watch daily and wait for them to drop, and we gather them quickly as all the floodplain's fruit-loving creatures will want them as well.

It took a year or two to figure out that the fruit never turns any color besides dull green. When they hit the ground you just need to trust they're ripe and bite a hole in the skin and suck all the sweet yellow pulp out, and sort the big shiny seeds with your tongue to spit back into the undergrowth. Pawpaws, like fall grapes, are not for dainty eaters, the faint of heart about seeds and spitting.

You're not likely to see pawpaws at the Farmers' Market. The fruit's perishable once it drops off the tree, and it doesn't travel well. It's best to eat it where you find it, as often as you find it.

Several years after we discovered the pawpaw patch by the creek we grew ambitious. A bumper yield of pawpaws made it possible to bring a bag home and squeeze the yellow pulp out and separate the flat black seeds (like a persimmon), add a little orange juice and some ice, and blend the whole mess up for smoothies. "A poor man's banana," Betsy called them as we convinced our boys to give our concoction a try. They sipped and said they prefer real bananas, but I'm happy they can at least say that in their boyhoods they ate off the land.

Some say a ripe pawpaw tastes more like a mango, and I like the comparison since it summons that tropical touch I associate with the leaves. There are many other more common wild fruits, berries, and nuts you could eat or prepare from the Piedmont woods— the black cherry, the elderberry, the white mulberry, blackberries, persimmons—but the pawpaw is the one that always catches my wild-food imagination this time of year.

—September 1, 2006

Backyard Habitat

I don't spend much time channel surfing, but the other morning I was stuck in the house waiting for the cable man, and I wandered into a program on Animal Planet called *Backyard Habitat*. I'll admit: I was fascinated. On the program, a perky former Miss Florida in khaki pedal pushers and a friendly naturalist from the National Wildlife Federation fly all over the country helping families revamp their old-style yards into little pieces of territory friendly to wildlife. It's a sort of "Green Eye for the Normal Guy."

In an hour I witnessed a suburban backyard in central Florida turned into a bird sanctuary, and another on the edge of a state park in Washington State revamped into a pond garden fit for burrowing mountain beavers and ring-neck pigeons. Each backyard makeover included selected special projects fit for your spot, such as moss birdhouses, hanging stale-bagel feeders covered with peanut butter, tadpole observatories, and mockingbird piazzas.

Habitat for wildlife, the naturalist host points out often during the program, has four essential factors: cover, food, water, and safe places to nest and raise young. When the *Backyard Habitat* crew moves in, yards usually don't provide these four factors in much abundance. It's fascinating, though, how by shifting a few aesthetic suburban priorities, it's easy to create good territory for wildlife right under all our noses.

And what needs to change if backyards are to become better habitat? Keeping all the grass cut an inch high might be good for putting or kicking a soccer ball, but it is not good habitat for wildlife. An ecologist friend of mine looks out at the greenswards of suburbia and calls them "a vast green desert." Not much lives in a lawn, and what tries to is eradicated with chemicals.

That perfectly clipped green moustache of same-species shrubbery planted around the house does not make good habitat either. Diversity is the key in creating habitat. A variety of native plants makes for better cover and wildlife feeding than the relatively short list of conventional plants we usually purchase and use in our yards.

The crew for *Backyard Habitat* almost always suggests installing a water feature somewhere as well. For the Florida family it was a small jar of bubbling water that drained into a base of cobblestones. This provided enough flowing water to add an element of sound to their backyard, but the top of the jar also offered a small pool for birds to get a drink on a hot Florida day.

In Washington State, the land of the burrowing mountain beavers, the family requested a larger pond, and so the *Habitat* crew dug a wide hole, lined it with black plastic, and brought in a load of rock to create a formidable water feature, a real watering hole fit for bringing in the bigger, wilder game from the surrounding state park.

When the two hosts of *Backyard Habitat* finished with these two yards, they presented each family with a certificate from the National Wildlife Federation, stating its spots on the planet as fully made-over and certified them as "Backyard Habitat[s]." They also left a rock behind with the show's official logo on it.

Of course, all this got me thinking about our own backyard. After the cable man finally showed up, I spent an hour walking around, looking for the four magic elements of habitat. I'm glad I found them everywhere around me.

Most of the space around our house is Piedmont hardwood forest, deep and untended. There's no need to do anything to this forest to make it better habitat. It's been pretty good natural habitat for tens of thousands of years.

Closer to the house, it's great to sit on a little bamboo bench and watch the green and brown anoles prowl through the pitcher plants and blue flag iris. Our bog habitat is a sort of fast-food haven for lizards. When I look inside the barrels of the pitcher plants (native to bogs in the Carolina coastal plain) I often see an insect slowly decomposing. Add a bog to your yard, and it's the plants themselves that can be seen as the predators.

On the west side of the house we have two small ponds. They are full of frogs, and this week there were three white leathery eggshells left behind on the edge of one of them where turtles or snakes had hatched out. The upper pond has supported a small population of bream and minnows for two years now, and once I saw a heron sorting through the lilies for breakfast. I don't feel as compelled to protect these native fish as I would expensive showy koi. I let the bream fend for themselves. I just restock from the creek every spring.

So why create habitat for wildlife? "Imagine a child growing up without having the opportunity to watch a tadpole changing into a frog, to smell a wildflower, or to wade in a clear stream," the creators of *Backyard Habitat* ask us to consider. The pressure on wild places and the creatures that live in them is greater today than ever before. "Natural habitat is disappearing at an alarming rate, and habitat loss is the number one threat to wildlife today."

Go out and take an inventory of your own backyard. Is your yard habitat, or is it part of Lawn Planet, the vast "green desert" stretching all across America?

—September 15, 2006

Migration Station

For the last two weeks I've been seeing the monarchs migrating through. No, I don't mean that convoys of kings and queens have been trucking down the interstate. I'm talking about the most royal of butterflies, the orange, black, and white monarch.

Monarchs share the Upstate with many butterflies: the brown skippers, the yellow-green sulphurs, the yellow and black and the blue and black swallowtails and others. The monarchs could be the most beautiful of them all, but it's their life cycle and not their beauty that intrigues me most. They're part of a group called "the milkweed butterflies" because of the plant that the larvae like to feed on. Milkweed makes them taste disagreeable to birds, and so they have a natural protection from these predators. The adults feed on other nectars, but the milkweed keeps them safe from birds for life.

Lately as I've been sitting on the screened porch in the afternoons I've seen the monarchs appear from up the driveway (north) and park for a sip of nectar on the aptly-named butterfly bushes in the side yard, and then flit off into the woods behind us. I know they're headed south to their wintering grounds far away. It's gratifying to have them stop for a snack in my backyard.

It's quite a journey they have ahead of them. All the monarchs east of the Rockies fly 3,000 miles to the mountains of Mexico.

(West of the Rocky Mountains the monarchs don't have quite as far to go—they migrate to California.) Those that fly south spend the winter and fly back north in the spring to lay their eggs. After three generations of summer butterflies have come and gone, the last generation heads back south. The remarkable migration of the monarchs is "more like birds or whales," one field guide reports.

Sitting at a football game on Saturday, most in the stadium were focused on the action down at field level. I was watching the sky above, counting monarchs as they moved through, oblivious to the score. Like a good running back, they had their shoulders squared and were headed north-south. By the time the fourth quarter had rolled around I had seen twenty-two monarch butterflies and that was just on my side of the field. I tried to do the math and multiply these travelers by every acre of the Piedmont, but it was too many butterflies to imagine.

It's possible to miss this grand butterfly show if you're down at ground level and caught in a snarl of human concerns. Some years I'll look up one day in late September or early October and see a single monarch straggling past and say, "I've missed it." Other years, if I time it right, I find a high place on the nearby mountain front right at the peak of the migration, and it's possible to see thousands of the butterflies moving past. In a high place, you can focus your binoculars on the migration and pick out butterflies to what seems infinity. They're not all monarchs, but many of them are. It's more exciting than a homecoming parade.

Some years I make it up to see the grand parade on the mountain front and sometimes I don't. No matter what, it wouldn't be fall for me without the monarchs and their migration. I'm always looking to the natural cycles for inspiration and wisdom. I find it in the waves of animals coming and going, the seasonal changes, the ups and downs.

Fall is always the most reflective of times. Maybe it's the temperature plunging, but for whatever reason, it's this time of year I always start thinking big. I'm not the first to do this. Alison

Hawthorne Deming has a whole book of poetry called *The Monarchs*. It's a sixty-poem sequence inspired by the migration of the butterflies. "Sleep, Monarchs, rising and falling/with the wind, orange children tucked in your winter bed,/teachers of patience and faith," Deming says in one of her last poems in the sequence.

So monarchs migrating are a metaphor for something larger. They teach us "patience and faith," they teach us how to live even our own brief but "purpose-driven" lives. Noting the passing of the monarchs each year reminds me how to pay attention, how something as small as a butterfly can be both fragile and strong.

Seeing the monarchs migrating each year makes me feel attached to what eco-philosopher David Abram has called "the more-than-human world." No matter how hard we humans try to level everything—temperature, landscape, playing fields—migrating butterflies remind me we're all part of the rounded year, the process of change, what used to be called "the great chain of being."

A lepidopterist: that's what they call someone who studies butterflies. Alive and aware: that's what I feel when I note these colorful vagrants as they pass through in the fall.

—October 6, 2006

Ode to a Truck

I'd like to observe a moment of silence for the passing of all the beloved and never-to-be-forgotten automobiles through my life. Excuse me while I indulge in a spot of quiet reflection for the many masses of metal, plastic, rubber, and glass I've owned, serviced, traded in or sold in my thirty-five years of driving.

Indulge me as I remember my first car, a baby-blue 1963 Ford Falcon coupe with bucket seats I bought for 500 hard-earned dollars and lost soon after when someone ran the traffic light at Glendalyn and Pine and sideswiped me on the way home from school in 1970.

And then there was the 1968 Volkswagen Beetle I drove through high school and college. (I paid $500 for that one too.) It had a deeply dented hood I never fixed, the windshield wipers didn't work half the time, the alternator was bad, and I had to park on a hill so I could always get a good run at a jump start. Praised be the 100,000 miles we drove together through my youth.

Praise to my first new car, a white 1976 Datsun B-210, with thirty-six monthly payments of $130 in a coupon book. I paid that one off, then sold it in Seattle during the 1979 oil crisis for $100 more than it cost. I rode a bicycle through the high gas prices of the next two years.

Coming home in 1983 I remember the worthless 1970 red Toyota I bought for $700, what seemed to me like a fortune at the time. It burned so much oil I looked like a rolling oil rig fire. I hated that car, but when I got a job it carried me to work. In 1984 some generous car dealer at the Mazda dealership took it as a trade on a new blue four-door GLC. I bought racks for that one and it became my first paddling car. I kept my two kayaks tied to the top through all four seasons.

In 1988 I took a teaching job at Wofford and bought my first truck, a grey Mazda. That summer I put a camper top on the back. The idea was that I could pack everything I owned of value in the bed. The first summer I strapped on my boat and my bike, and I drove across country and back, and not one mile of it on an interstate highway. I was gone two months and I drove over 6,000 miles on two-lanes, some dirt, many paved. I slept in the bed. I ate strawberry rhubarb pie every day in some local diner.

All this is prelude for the passing of my latest vehicle. Last week I traded in my dark blue Toyota 4x4 pickup for a new grey GMC 4x4 Canyon. I've come to like the idea that I'm now driving a GMC pickup truck, a vehicle Jerry Jeff Walker immortalized in his famous song "Up Against the Wall Redneck Mothers."

I bought the Toyota in 1994. By then I'd settled down, and my possessions wouldn't fit in a tractor trailer, much less a pickup. Prosperity had set in, and I'd bought a little cabin in the mountains. My neighbor had already pulled my Mazda out with his tractor. "You need a 4x4 if you're coming up here in the winter," Mr. Marsh observed from the high seat of his John Deere. I went home and bought my Toyota.

The summer of 1994 I had high hopes that I would become one of those guys in the commercials—a member of the 200,000-mile club. By last week I'd made it to 170,000, but the old truck was burning lots of oil, the clutch was slipping, and the radiator had a leak. My friend Lee Hagglund had almost totaled it in 1995 on some black ice in Vermont. In 1997 a hail storm dented the hood, and in

2003 a crepe myrtle stove in the back quarter panel a little bit, but not enough to get it fixed.

The truck was paid for a decade ago, and last week I finally knew it was time to give in to that All-American impulse—buy a new car, smell that new car smell, and feel the pride of a credit check. "This will make somebody a good huntin' truck," the guys at the GMC showroom said as they calculated my trade-in.

Let me stop here and take the criticism head-on: I know Mr. Kudzu Telegraph should have bought a hybrid, but I just couldn't do it. I'm a truck guy, and Mr. Marsh no longer has his tractor. The best I could do this time about saving the planet was opt for the mid-size truck that promises 22 miles per gallon and vow to ride my bike more.

Any careful reader will also note that for the first time since 1968 I'm back in the domestic market. They'll also know that the distinction between "foreign" and "domestic" doesn't mean quite what it did thirty-five years ago. BMWs are now made in Spartanburg County, and Toyotas are assembled over in Tennessee. And brand loyalty? Family now is a much deeper current. I'm married into the car business, and so it only made sense I go to my GMC-dealer brother-in-law for my next vehicle. I trust he gave me a good deal. I know I'll get good service.

A decade from now I'll most likely be singing the praises of this GMC truck as it falls in line with all the other vehicles that have passed through my life. You might try this survey at home. Take a moment and write down in the margin of this column a list of all those vehicles that have complicated your finances. Think of them right now parked bumper to bumper in the street in front of your house. Write their year of production, their color, their model name. Think of how many good miles you've traveled, and all the places you've gone.

—October 13, 2006

The Battle for Sugar Tit

One night soon after I first returned to Spartanburg in 1988 I was sitting in a bar out near the Westgate Mall, and there was a guy next to me who wore his hair in a mullet and had boots made out of reptile skin. He still had that Marshall Tucker Band "Long Hard Ride" look going ten years after the album, and it was even topped off with a cowboy hat. His accent was deep and distinctive Piedmont South Carolina, a high-pitched drawl, a slow wash of regional inflection unaffected by TV or changing Upstate demographics.

It was Friday night. I listened as he made his first move on a pretty young woman who happened to sit down next to him. After she'd settled in, the good ole boy turned her way and said, "So, you on city water or you got your own well?"

I don't remember what she answered, but I've never forgotten the question. I've used it for years to help define the deep fault lines between city and county here where I live. Some people laugh and get it right away. For others I have to explain: my man at the bar wasn't fishing only for companionship. He was asserting how the rural culture of independence in Spartanburg County can be defined by things most of us now take for granted. Even in the rituals of courtship he was unwilling to give up the most basic of services— water in this case—to control by "the man" back in the city. In 1988 there was still a place called country, and he was still a country boy. He hoped to push those values into the next generation.

I've been thinking about this incident for weeks and wondering whether he was from Sugar Tit. He surely would understand the current complex modern struggle between that little former farming community and the sprawling Interstate 85 corridor "city" of Greer a few miles to its north and west.

Maybe twenty years ago that woman he talked to in the bar answered, "I got my own well," and they danced all night at a little place he knew down near Walnut Grove, and months later they got married in Gatlinburg and moved into an old tenant house or a trailer out near the Enoree River.

Maybe when his daddy died they finally got title to a flat ten acres of land that used to be a cotton field plowed with a mule by his granddaddy but gone now to gullies and pine trees. Maybe his two brothers got ten acres each as well right down Highway 101.

Our man hunted deer in the fall right near the house, and his wife was involved with their local church and worked at the local hospital system as a nurse's aide. Maybe their kids ended up at Woodruff High and played in the band just as he did twenty-five years earlier.

They liked the rural life out in Sugar Tit, and they didn't want to see it go, but maybe that ten acres in the next twenty years quickly became a subdivision waiting to happen in the imagination of some sharp-tongued, deep-pocketed developer driving an SUV who thought he could talk our county boy out of his granddaddy's land. All that developer needed was some wannabe "city" like Greer to push gas, water, and cable down this ole boy's road that dead-ends at the river, and he could make a killing.

That developer knew that if he could just get every good ole boy from Woodruff to Sugar Tit to sell him ten acres he could turn that whole corner of Spartanburg County into a place that looks like Pelham over in Greenville, miles and miles of tract homes, lawns, and a Wal-Mart or a Publix or two in the mix as well.

City water is just the start of it. After "basic services" you get pavement instead of gravel drives, lawn care, curbs, sidewalks, ordinances, taxes, stoplights, crepe myrtles instead of chinaberry trees, Jack Russell Terriers instead of beagles, and subdivision after subdivision with names like Deer Track, Forest Oaks, Well Spring, and Meadow Brook where once was Sugar Tit.

Well, I'd be willing to bet that good ole boy still doesn't want that city water pushing out in his direction. He still likes his well water, even though he could use the money the developer's offering, since BMW was never hiring his kind anyway.

I'm pulling for the Sugar Tits of the world against Greer. If Sugar Tit goes, where will it all stop? Is our man from Sugar Tit wrong for wanting to hang on to the old Southern rural way? Should every rural Southern place be plowed over by market forces? In a hundred years will every square inch of our rural South be subdivided and settled into grids of good roads, sewer lines, and subdivisions?

I've been on city water all my life, but deep down inside I've always wanted my own well.

—October 20, 2006

Winter Is A-Coming in

We're officially not-quite-halfway between autumn equinox on September 21st and winter solstice on December 21st, but the "cold alert" has been sounding in our house for the last week or so. We've had a frost, the leaves are falling, and the heat's even kicked on two or three times.

My wife, Betsy, looks to the mercury creeping downward as a time to mourn the passing of deep Southern summer. She puts her warm-weather clothes away with reluctance and savors every temporary rise in temperatures, hoping that this year maybe the cold will just pass us by.

There's so much to keep up with when it's cold. We have a fireplace and there are wood piles to maintain. Out in the side yard is the big one, but we keep some stacked on the front porch for easy access. There's shuttling the wood back and forth in the wheel barrow between them. There are ashes to empty when it burns and wood to bring in for the next one. We've already had one fire. It was earlier this year than last by a week. The first fire each year is an important event. It marks the boundary between warm and cold.

Just this week we were heading up to the mountains for an annual October weekend with friends. Our place there sits at 3,000 feet and winter's about three weeks earlier than it is here. The trees are already bare and the wind whips around. Before we left, Betsy fished last winter's gloves out of the closet and found only five odd pairs. There was one full set, from two different ski gloves, but she wore them anyway, along with a floppy black hat.

I take to the cold. I like making an inventory of bulky socks and buying more each year if I need them. I like wearing long pants again and layering flannel shirts and old reliable jackets. The cold is the only time of the year you'll see me in a sport coat, usually a gold corduroy one with elbow patches like we joke college professors always wear.

Getting out my outdoor clothes deepens my fondness for the seasons as well. Every item engineered for warmth and comfort outdoors tells a story of my years in the woods and on the rivers. I still wear the dark blue Patagonia jacket I've had for twenty-two years. Rather than buy a new one, I've sent this one back two times for new zippers. That ancient jacket reminds me of two decades of winter. There are burn holes from campfires and stains from cooking in gloves.

Fall is my favorite time of the year. I like the seams of experience it reveals, the need for passages, the way the cooling evenings point out where we were and where we're going. July is absorbent. Experiences disappear into its long days and bloom. In October things fall away and the distances are revealed.

October is a reflective month. On days like this, I think about the planet in motion, and the winter is where we naturally head after the deep warmth of summer's growing season. I don't know if I could live in a place where there were not distinct seasons.

Yet there is something sad about all the falling away around us after October has passed. The November trees have dropped their leaves, the water cools, the vines, so bold and expansive in July, all die back. By December everything begins to move indoors. Things are put away—gardens, shorts, hoses, and sandals. By the time January rolls around you have to listen very carefully in the slumbering depths of winter to hear the sound of April approaching.

Far north in Montreal it's said there's an entire city underground, with a constant temperature of seventy degrees. People there can go from home to work and back every day and never step outside. They can shop, go to movies, eat dinner in a restaurant and never have to step up on the surface of our bitter cold planet. We have it better here. Sometimes in winter a warm snap will remind us how far south we really are. Winter for us is often more of a concept than a reality.

I know there are places close to the equator where it never gets cold, where the eternal breeze is the temperature of July, the attitude is tropical, and the trees are palms. Gloves are foreign objects there. These are not the places of my dreams. I need the changes that arrive on the solstices and equinoxes in October, December, March, and June. I need the four points on the earth's compass.

In my religion one of the sacraments has always been this yearly change, this natural system of seasons. My faith is in cycles. I look to the shortening days for strength and assurance. The warmth will come back around and I wait it out.

—October 27, 2006

Into the Wild

One of the most complex films of the year opened in the area last week. No, it's not another *Spiderman* remake or Adam Sandler comedy with adolescent slapstick humor. This one's about adolescent longing. There's no sex, very few drugs, and the only rock and roll is Eddie Vedder's soulful sound track.

Director Sean Penn's *Into the Wild* is a beautiful exploration of the sloppy search for adolescent freedom and transcendence, its rewards and risks. It's based on a true story documented by John Krakauer's best-selling book by the same title. You might have at least heard the plot line by now: Soon after graduating from Emory University, privileged Chris McCandless gives his $24,000 trust fund to Oxfam, drives west, leaves his old Toyota abandoned off-road, burns his last few hundreds of dollars, bums around channeling the literary ghosts of Jack Kerouac and Jack London, paddles the Colorado River, and finally heads north, "into the wild," to discover the meaning of life among big mountains.

After that, things turn both good and bad. Chris (who took the road name "Alexander Supertramp") screws up and can't ford a glacial river to walk out when he's ready to return to civilization. He starves, tries foraging for food, reads the field guide wrong, and eats a wild plant that kills him. Chris/Alex ends up dying, filled with light, in an old city bus somebody's hauled into the woods for a hunting cabin.

In the end, he's staring at the sky, looking for a transcendence he's searched for since childhood in literature and experience. Like so many careless artists and searchers, he dies in his early twenties. His body is later found by moose hunters, and his sister flies his ashes home.

Director Sean Penn is the master of little things: early on, an entire contemporary poem is recited on-screen. When else has that happened in an American film? And later, a whole paragraph of Leo Tolstoy appears on-screen from a story Chris is reading in the bus to gain enlightenment. When was the last time "text" was a minor character in any film? It's enough to make an English professor proud.

There are wonderful animal moments too: gulls playing in the waves on an isolated beach, birds in endless sky, caribou in Alaska, a fly-blown moose carcass, even a grizzly bear visitor to camp—all postcards from the "more-than-human world" you'd expect in a film about wildness.

I always tell my beginning literature students not to neglect pondering the title, and in this case it's a big fat finger pointing to the story's theme.

Examining "wildness" is the point of this film, and the search for it is something you usually see Hollywood directors exploring in cities through murder, greed, graft, illicit sex, and swindling, good American anti-values.

On a personal level, I saw my own idealistic wasted youth spattered across the screen in vivid colors. (Hello, my name is John and I too wanted at twenty-two to walk "into the wild" and act as if I had no past or future.)

I'm glad I didn't walk quite as far in as Chris McCandless. I'm glad I didn't end up dead in a bus in Alaska. But I think I could have. I like it when a film shows another possible me that I somehow bypassed. I was inches away a dozen times from being Chris. But

I never went that far "into the wild." Don't many of us have that storyline?

Penn seems to be saying we'd be better off as a society if everyone found his own "wild" and explored his connections to life as Chris did. I think had things not gone bad, Chris would have come back out and taken his place among us. He would have made up with his family and gotten a job. But in a story they say only conflict is interesting, so it didn't work out that way.

Chris might have been able to read Tolstoy, but he had serious trouble with his field guide to edible plants. After college, he made an "A" in Enlightenment, but failed Natural History. His average grade is "C minus." His mistakes killed him. His story makes us think about all the bullets we've dodged. Go see the film and decide whether Chris McCandless is an idiot or a hero. I see him as both, embodying a necessary tension in life.

—November 24, 2006

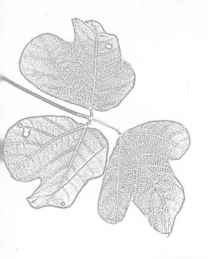

Venison Tacos

I've been thinking about hunting all week. Thanksgiving morning we woke up to shooting on two sides. For a half-hour or so it sounded like a Baghdad firefight. Upstream, to our west, ducks and geese were probably falling in a series of shotgun volleys, and to the east, downstream, somebody else had mounted his tree stand to shoot a few holiday rounds at some of South Carolina's estimated 900,000 deer in the dawn's early light.

Most people who don't hunt live their lives in cities or neighborhoods where hunting can easily become an abstraction. We don't have that luxury. Though we live only three and a half miles from Morgan Square, gunshots are not unusual out here on the "Lower Eastside." We're barely out in the county, and the area is still blessed with large privately-owned tracts of undeveloped land on both sides of the creek. The view from our deck is out into a long finger of timbered wilderness pointing toward the asphalt reaches of the urban core.

These seasonal discharges of ammunition assure us the bulldozers or logging skidders aren't coming to our backyard any time soon. Wild land in the South has always meant hunting land. The owners of the land around us are avid hunters, people who care deeply about maintaining stretches of landscape suitable for their sport.

But that's not what I've been thinking about. What I've really been thinking about is why I don't hunt, why I'm not one of the men or women who will bag the 300,000 deer this hunting season. In relation to this I've also been thinking about where we get our meat from and whether I can continue to eat pork and beef and chickens produced in industrial feed lots and hog sheds and poultry houses.

So, I'll take one complex personal issue at a time. Why don't I hunt? I don't know exactly. Maybe it's about having guns around. Even when I've been given a shotgun or a .22, as has happened several times in my life, I've had no desire to keep them, care for them, shoot them, smell gun smoke, or listen to the discharge. I've quickly passed them on to someone who will love them. Guns have never interested me much, and it's hard to develop a joy in modern hunting without an interest in guns.

Is my lack of interest in guns why I don't hunt? Well, not really. I know there's always bow-hunting, or even the archaic art of the throwing stick, the atlatal. I could take these up and go into the woods. But I don't think my not hunting is really about my lack of interest in guns.

I have friends who are hunters with guns—some of them environmental writers—and I know they turn their seasonal outings into rituals and make the killing of deer and birds as quick and humane as possible. I know there is skill and art involved in being a good hunter, and I like ritual and skill and art. So why not hunt?

Come to think of it, it's not the hunting that I don't like. I have "hunted" all my life. I've walked hundreds of miles in search of snakes and birds in a dozen different countries. Actually, I've been pretty good at hunting, at surprising snakes on the edge of a field and catching them, at locating rare birds among brush. I have just hunted with binoculars and snake sticks.

It's really the killing and not the hunting that keeps me from joining up. It's the reality of bringing a fellow creature's life to an end that has always stopped me short of shooting at something. Mostly my not hunting with guns is about having no desire to kill the few wild things I have the privilege to encounter.

I know there are too many deer in the state, but I don't see too many. I like to watch deer move among us. I enjoy thwarting their browsing in the yard by planting deer-resistant shrubs.

But hunt them? You've got to remember I'm one of those guys who keeps a plastic cup on the screened porch so I can remove the yellow jackets caught inside. I drive slower than needed around curves because I know from past experience that there might be some fellow creature—frog, turtle, snake, raccoon, possum, fox, deer—crossing the road, and I think it's my responsibility to avoid killing them.

I don't like killing wild things, but I do enjoy eating meat, so I know somebody's got to kill what we eat. In our family we're not vegetarian, and there's not much discussion of converting. We eat meat, and so I feel responsible about where it comes from. I've been experimenting a little lately with free-range chickens and pork and beef produced organically. It's one solution to the problem of industrial meat production, but a hard one at this point to maintain, especially if you eat out in restaurants where bottom-line costs rule everything.

And that brings me to the venison tacos. Last night for one meal we avoided eating meat raised in the obscene conditions of an industrial beef or hog or chicken operation because my brother-in-law, a hunter, opened his family larder and gave us a pound of dark red venison wrapped in white butcher paper. The week before, he'd loaded up his freezer with the carved-up bodies of two Piedmont deer he'd shot. He passed the wild bounty on, and we ate. For a few hours I didn't worry about where our food came from, but I also didn't have to kill it. It was a good arrangement.

—December 1, 2006

Riding the Hogback Highway

This week we drove U.S. Highway 176 north to Landrum three days in a row to watch our son play in a basketball tournament at the new District 1 high school. We could have driven the faster, more sterile I-26, but taking the old highway has its advantages and insights.

I like to call this route the "Hogback Highway" because anywhere west of town along its length you might just catch a glimpse of old Hogback Mountain. Until the construction of the Denny's building downtown, Hogback was the most significant vertical feature in the Spartanburg region.

In the early days before interstates, all travelers would have been aware of their relation to Hogback's 3,240-foot ridge looming on the escarpment thirty miles distant. Now that farming's no longer our primary industry there are more trees. Hogback's harder to see. There are probably people who don't even know it exists, this blue ghost looming above Landrum, judging our every human action.

Driving the Hogback Highway is an exercise in landscape perspective and time travel. In twenty miles the road cuts across every era of Spartanburg's history, from the old market town's surviving nineteenth-century Morgan Square, to Hub City's Southern Shops where the old trains were repaired, to I-85's now faded mid-twentieth-century New South optimism, on up into to the deep rural western corner of the county now under serious threat from twenty-first-century California-style condo-sprawl.

It would have been a great deal more pleasant to drive out I-585, the four-lane interstate gateway out of town, past the kept industrial grounds and ponds of Milliken & Company and the institutional fountains of USC-Upstate. But instead we drove U.S. 176 through the blight of Asheville Highway because I wanted to feel it full in my face.

Does anyone on our County Council ever drive the stretch of highway between Cleveland Park and Business I-85 and feel guilty for the sins and omissions of councils past? Is this what former farm fields must look like when the invisible hand of the free market passes over? Is the ugliness and clutter of Asheville Highway merely the "collateral damage" of late twentieth-century capitalism? Who can look now on what happened on Asheville Highway in the 1970s and 1980s and call it good?

Drive up U.S. 176 over the new I-85 and you see another past failure of political will and oversight. There's an Ingle's shopping center on the right with few canopy trees and little required buffer for the 1970s subdivision behind it. Just across the road a Winn-Dixie shopping center stands empty and abandoned. Who can look at what the free market did here in the last decade of the twentieth century at this former rural crossroads and call it progress?

The old mill town of Inman didn't fare much better. The whole strip along U.S. 176 is a snarl of uncontrolled signs, cheap buildings, oversized asphalt parking lots, and abandoned husks of businesses that didn't make it. Who can call this good?

It's not until you get up toward Gramling that Hogback country begins to take on its true beauty. There the mountain stands bold and tall over rolling countryside. It's still rural there. If only there were sheep it might look like rural England. The old agricultural character of Spartanburg County survives there in the shadow of Hogback. If County Council has a conscience it will take this little rural patch of Spartanburg County and replicate it through planning and land use regulations from Pacolet to Landrum, from Sugar Tit to Cowpens.

Forget the silliness of arguing over a road tax. Abandon the short-sighted idea of selling off our park land. Maybe somebody should rent County Council a van and drive the whole gang up Highway 176 to Gramling, bring along a bag lunch, and talk about what they see along the way: the good, the bad, and the ugly.

Then they can set about planning how it will come to pass that some stretches of our county will still look like that spot in one hundred years. Maybe in the shadow of Hogback they'll have a place-based conversion, pass a $25 "save our county" tax, and pledge to pay people market value for key pieces of rural landscape we need to preserve. That would show some progress.

It's time for a change. For over 200 years Hogback's watched how humans have moved below it with no plan, no regard for the beauty of this special landscape, governed mostly by those without much vision, led by few, driven by greed and self-interest.

—January 5, 2007

Small and Smaller

My writer/activist friend Janisse Ray has recently written an essay called "Bleeding Fields," all about rural exodus in the South. Janisse grew up in Baxley, a small farming town in south Georgia. Though she wasn't brought up on a farm (her father ran a junkyard), her grandparents were still on the land just outside of town all through her girlhood. She grew up eating homegrown okra and tomatoes. She knew the smell of tilled fields, could recognize a chicken shack and a mule. She grew up believing in small communities like Baxley and the surrounding rural culture that supported them.

But so much has changed so fast her head is spinning. In the leveling world of statistics, communities of fewer than 2,500 are considered rural, and only twenty-six percent of Southerners can now be classified that way. To be urban is now the norm, even in the South, a place whose myths and values are rooted deeply in fields and on farms.

"My current sadness is my chronic sadness," Janisse writes. "A way of life is passing, I have watched its passage, it is one I loved, and I am not sure that in my lifetime we will get it back."

I would argue that not only the rural is passing. Small is passing, too. To be small is disappearing. Small schools. Small communities. All gone to consolidation or growth brought on by believing in "economies of scale." We're losing it all to growth. If small is beautiful, as E. F. Schumacher said in his famous 1973 book, then there is less and less beauty every day in the South we love.

Janisse's essay got me thinking about our own situation right here in the Upcountry. We're growing fast and change is all around us. Will Spartanburg retain any small town character with Greenville growing into a real city so fast right next door? Will Anderson, Landrum, and Walhalla retain any of the culture associated with smallness? In the next fifty years, will even smaller places like Jonesville, Fountain Inn, Lockhart, and Dacusville empty out, or simply be steamrolled by suburbs from Greenville and Spartanburg?

This isn't the first time that a way of life has passed. We're now living on the cusp of a fourth great cultural collapse here in the upper South. First the stable world of native cultures disappeared with the coming of the Spanish in the 1540s; then, 400 hundred years later, Europeans had farmed out the land and the great rural exodus began that Janisse mourns.

Then an industrial culture came and went like a flash. Mills and mill towns were built, worked, abandoned and in many cases salvaged in a little over a hundred years. It's hard to believe something can come and go so fast. All that's left in many cases are family memories of working in a mill and the fortunes these mills made their owners.

So the history of the South has always been one of cultural collapse. "After the lapse of 500 sometimes catastrophic years [since the arrival of Europeans]," environmental historian Albert Cowdrey argues, "it is hard to say which is more remarkable, that so much has changed in the southern landscape, or that so much remains the same."

I know none of this reflection helps with the current pain of small places being eaten up by larger ones. There are small towns all over the region struggling with consolidation. There are small-scale schools being eaten by larger ones because districts might save some money. Nothing soothes the pain when your old school closes or your grandparents' small farm is sold and bulldozed for the next strip mall or mega high school or distribution plant or subdivision.

The larger question is what we can do about it. What is the new culture we are now building on the ruins of the earlier ones? Will the service culture of hospitals and schools and fast food last? Will suburban culture endure once gas is no longer cheap or plentiful? How will we make a living here amidst the great I-85/I-26 sprawl in fifty years? "The South is at a crossroads," Janisse writes. "An old farmer on a tractor is driving along a Southern highway, down a long hill, and he is passed by a log truck [and then] a queue of city bicyclists in skintight spandex." Where do we fall in line?

—February 2, 2007

The Mighty Chinquapin

When I was a kid growing up on the north side of Spartanburg one of the AM radio stations I listened to claimed to broadcast "from the banks of the mighty Chinquapin." It made Chinquapin Creek, the largest of Lawson's Fork's tributaries, sound like the Mississippi River.

I think that radio announcer's humor might have been the beginning of my fascination with local streams. As I listened to the radio it didn't matter that by the early 1960s there wasn't much wild or natural about the Chinquapin below where it crossed under I-85. It didn't matter that it was already compromised and channeled by progress along I-585 and North Pine Street, or that the newly built Pinewood Shopping Center drained acres of asphalt directly into it, or that it ran right past a recently closed and capped early city dump. It didn't matter that Chinquapin Creek was polluted by Beaumont Mill, or by "Gas Bottom." It didn't matter that by the 1960s there was far more kudzu than chinquapin oak along its length. What mattered to me was that it lived and survived in my imagination.

It wasn't only the imaginary "mighty Chinquapin" I knew. We lived for several years just uphill from the creek, and I played in the real Chinquapin's narrow channel catching crayfish and those little fish Southerners call knotty heads. When I was eight or nine years old that little creek had been my "nearby nature." Almost every afternoon I wandered down from Florida Avenue (up behind where the Dodge dealership now operates), crossed a cleared field, and descended into what I now know was the remnants of an empty reservoir, the source of Spartanburg's first water supply.

There was a leftover concrete buttress of a dam down in there, and it looked to a child like a Roman ruin. I could walk along the creek with I-585 out of sight above me and pretend it was the Amazon, or the Wild West. Thank goodness I grew up before video games. I might have stayed home. Today I might not have even noticed the Chinquapin (or the radio) existed.

But that's enough nostalgia for the good old days of my youth. I started out meaning to tell you about a hike I took last Friday on the upper Chinquapin right below where it crosses under I-85. It was cold when I met Spartanburg Area Conservancy's Mary Walter and Fred Parrish, and Palmetto Conservation Foundation's expert trail builder Jim Majors on what will soon be the next preserve for the Spartanburg Area Conservancy (SPACE).

Last year the South Carolina Conservation Bank granted SPACE $692,000 to buy forty-one acres of wetland and ridge from a willing landowner along the creek, and in partnership with PCF they are establishing a trail system though the property. It seems the mighty Chinquapin is finally getting its due.

On Friday we walked downstream, crossing and recrossing the narrow but bold creek where footbridges will be built. There are some big hardwoods in the Chinquapin bottom and some have grown into a strange swirling pattern Fred calls "that twisted canopy of the seepage forest." Winter birds flitted in and out of the underbrush as we walked, and once a cardinal so bright red it looked like a finger of flame sat in a bare dogwood and sang sharp and clear.

Walking the new Chinquapin trails, it's possible to forget the twenty-first century, the twentieth century, even the nineteenth century when the Scots-Irish settled this land for better or worse. It's possible to forget, as I did when I was a child, that I-585 is only a few hundred yards off to the east, funneling traffic toward the busy city center, or that there's a huge American flag flapping at the Milliken Research Park.

Before I forget the twenty-first century, though, it's good to always remember that this is the century of easements and greenways and conservation banks and recovered wild land like the Chinquapin Preserve, saved from a second settlement, slipped out of the grasp of the market economy and reserved for those like us who like to stroll in the territory of the cardinal, the fox, the deer, and the heron.

I hope there will be more willing landowners ready to preserve land, especially along our abundant creeks and rivers. The mighty Chinquapin runs forever through my imagination, and now a passage of it runs protected through the north side of Spartanburg.

—February 23, 2007

Approaching Frog
and Maple Time

I've always been tuned in to the big rolling wheel of the seasons. I hold a deep reverence for things that move in cycles (most things), and so take any opportunity I can to direct attention to seasonal change. I'm always surprised when I realize that not everyone sees time as this deep cycle of millions of seasons (spring, summer, fall, winter without end) wheeling along from Big Bang to Eternity. Seasonal change is my baseline, my stock market, my creed, my insurance policy against meaninglessness and deep doubt.

So do me a favor and look and listen carefully this week, and I'll bet you will see and hear spring opening the rusty trap door and creeping back into the woods and yards around your house just as I do.

You might think this celebration is a little premature. After all, only a week ago it was deep South Carolina winter: twenty degrees and windy. The rhododendron leaves under our front window were curled tight against the branches. But on the big wheel of the seasons, winter has now almost rolled past. It's only a little over three weeks before spring officially arrives on March twenty-first.

For me, there are two leading heralds of the hopeful return of spring: the appearance of a misty red sheen in the woods and frog sounds. The tiny flowers of the common native red maples are just now emerging along the roadsides, and around here the frogs began calling several nights ago when the air turned a little warmer and heavy rain blew through the area.

We have plenty of red maples near us because we're next to the creek, and they may like the swamp forest in the floodplain most of all. They also grow up in abandoned fields, a first pioneer filling the space. I read that you can make maple syrup from their sap, though it has less sugar than their famous cousin, the far-North's sugar maple. If we did some sugaring down here it would be a little late for tapping. The maple sap's already risen, and the red flowers are already beginning to appear.

This is our fifth spring here, and each year the frogs have called in the river bottom behind our house. I've come to expect them, and welcome them, even celebrate their emergence. I wouldn't go as far as to call myself a worshipper of frogs, but I might say that I worship every spring at an altar they point toward: seasonal change. It's an ageless form of worship, and I count myself proudly still among its acolytes.

I've built three small ponds under our bedroom window to lure the frogs closer to the house. When it gets a little warmer we'll sleep with frogs of various types singing under the windows. They're not exactly hymns, but they'll do.

Frogs aren't like ducks and geese. They don't migrate through our holy land depending on the weather. They are resident spirits. They share the zip code through cold and warm weather. They've wintered over in the mud or wedged under rotting wood where it might be a little warmer. They emerge ready to celebrate and to love. The rains the last few days make it look like it could be a good frog year. The cycles seem to be holding. If I'd been born 3,000 years ago, I'd have been a contented druid watching my stone circle about now to see the equinox sun land where it did the year before and the year before that. I'm easily convinced by such observations, and I admire nature's complexity more than human nature's complications.

But I'm no Druid in spite of all this talk about frogs and maples and the sun's regular course. I'm a latter-day, twenty-first century Methodist-born skeptic with a weak spot for nature study and apocalypse. Last night *An Inconvenient Truth* won an Oscar for best documentary, and despite the hopeful singing of the frogs outside our window I worried about the end of the world I know and love, and how we're altering the seasonal patterns I love.

Davis Guggenheim and Al Gore's documentary exposes the convenient lie that we as a single species have no effect on the changing climate of our planet. Will that lie persist through the seasons of my lifetime?

—March 2, 2007

Home on the Range

We were out walking the dog last week when a neighbor pulled up and asked, "Any cows in your backyard?"

"Cows?"

"Two brown cows wandering around."

He explained how the cows had been grazing on the new grass down their way for two or three days and said we should keep an eye out for them in our end of the neighborhood. He'd seen them at least three times. We thanked him, and Betsy asked if he'd come and tell us if he saw them again. She didn't want to miss cows grazing in the suburbs.

As we walked home I remembered that I'd seen hoof prints on the trail by the creek, but I had assumed that somebody was back there riding horses. Suburban cows just weren't on my radar, though I knew there were some close by, across the creek off Country Club Road, and others up on Fernwood-Glendale Road. Why did it feel so strange? It wasn't as if we were in the middle of New York City.

I was amused, but Betsy was really excited. Living along the creek she'd seen some wildlife, but cows somehow were even better than deer or turkeys or a fox. Escaped cows seemed more exotic in Pierce Acres.

About 7 p.m. that evening our neighbor knocked on the door.

"The cows are down at the end of the street," he said.

Seeing is believing, so we jumped in the truck and cruised down to the intersection of Starline and Fairlane, and there they were: two brown cows calmly grazing in someone's front yard. They could have been in Iowa for all they cared. We didn't know whether to call the police or Ben & Jerry's.

I knocked on the front door. The people with the cows on their lawn weren't home. From their driveway I looked out over the yard and saw several deposits left by the cows and realized this neighbor wouldn't need to call Chemlawn this spring to fertilize. Soon the mini-herd was on the move, headed for greener lawns across the open range.

"Oh, no. Those cows are headed for Lake Forest Drive!" Betsy said, feeling like an urban cowgirl. "Use your truck to turn them back. Some teenager might plow into them out on the curve."

So I speeded up, and the cows speeded up, and before I knew it we were racing two brown cows up Fairlane. "Stampede!" I yelled out the window and slipped in front of them.

The cows responded when I yipped out the open window like Roy Rogers or Hoss Cartwright did in my TV youth. Their eyes grew large and alarmed. Then from a full gallop they turned and slipped through a gate and disappeared into the trees along the creek.

We haven't seen them since, though we look for them every day. We see hoof prints in the mud along the creek but have no idea if they are recent. It's as if the cows have disappeared back into the floodplain along the creek after one attempt to break out into the thick new grass of the suburbs.

In *Pilgrim at Tinker Creek*, Annie Dillard says that the cows she sees on her walks are "a human product like rayon ... like a field of shoes ...cast-iron shanks and tongues like foam insoles. You can't see through to their brains as you can with other animals; they have beef fat behind their eyes, beef stew."

Our insurgent cows are much more noble than that. Into their jailbreak from a steak and stew beef future I inject the will to live free and create their own destinies. I've imagined them like the buffalo that used to roam the Piedmont. I imagined these two brown cows like the last of the Mohicans, bringing wild ungulate energy back to Lawson's Fork.

At night I stand on the deck and listen for their mournful bellow from the woods. Cows on the lam. It doesn't get much better than this for a poet on the banks of Lawson's Fork.

—March 16, 2007

Spring Break

Last year over spring break I loaded up my canoe and headed for Columbia. It was a trip I'll never forget. We spent five nights on the river. I really felt like Huck Finn setting out for the territories. This year I'm catching up on all the yard work I've put off. I've discovered that our low-maintenance yard becomes high-maintenance if I don't do any at all.

So yesterday I launched spring holidays 2007 by weeding the gravel we used to replace the grass we didn't want to cut. It's labor intensive, but rewarding. I wiggle a strange U-shaped hoe back and forth under the weeds until they break loose. Then I rake this green invasion into a pile. When it's all said and done I still like the gravel better than a lawn, but I no longer believe the gravel is less work.

Then I faced the fact that the wildflower bed we planted three years ago over our septic field has to be reseeded and the grass needs to be removed. If I leave it alone it will quickly become what it really wants to be: an old field in succession. If I simply mow it then it will become what I don't want it to be—a lawn.

After that, I worked on the little series of garden ponds I've stocked with local bream and bass. A year's detritus was two inches deep on the bottoms, and I squatted on the edges and pulled out handful after handful of black, decomposing oak leaves. If I left them, after three or four years I'd have a series of bogs instead of ponds. Even something as simple as a small pond needs my help to stay what it is.

I think it's called the Second Law of Suburban Dynamics: without maintenance everything becomes something else. Gravel becomes lawn. Pond becomes bog. What is it with nature? Nothing stays what it is. Everything becomes something else over time.

So I looked around some more. This was just the first day of spring break. Should I weed the herb garden? (Herb garden becomes weed patch.) Should I replace the potted plants on the front porch? (Plant containers become catch basins for weed seeds.) Should I scrub the green sheen off the north-facing front porch that never gets any sun?

Should I spray the yellow pollen off the decks and walks? Betsy's nose tells her the pollen count in our yard this year might be approaching saturation. It's pretty nice living in a temperate zone, but treeless Arizona looks pretty good every year about this time when her allergies kick in. Leave the pollen on all the surfaces and it looks like we've had a yellow snowfall. Can't nature find a neater way to make more trees?

I looked around again. The leaves I didn't move last fall need removal from the beds so I can add this year's pine bark mulch. I pulled the blower out of the basement and plugged it in. I remembered that my friend Byron, a religion professor, says blowing leaves is in his top ten all-time favorite activities. He says when he retires he might just spend hours blowing leaves back and forth across his yard.

I haven't had enough practice with a leaf blower to really know how to use it with skill and accuracy, so I spend most of my time blowing them back from where they came. I've thought about asking Byron over for a beer and getting him to teach a quick workshop in the front yard—Leaf-blowing 101. I could set up my own little yard-work college of continuing education.

But maybe it's not my technique. Maybe it's the terrain. We don't have those vast expanses of suburban lawn where you can really get rafts of leaves moving across empty space. Trees, bushes, and rocks block the way every time I think I've got a good blow going.

Then I remember: it's spring break. I've got all week to work on stopping the yard entropy. Maybe when Byron comes over we'll just sit on the deck, drink that beer, and discuss the philosophical implications of forested lots and leaf-blowing, or whether yard work could be considered a religion, or if there is much chance a great literature will rise from these suburban meditations.

—April 6, 2007

Land-Use So an Alien Can
Understand It

I was out weeding my wildflower garden this week and, I kid you not, a spaceship landed. It was small and looked a little like an outdoor charcoal grill, all shiny and round. When it spoke I realized it was not an errant flying charcoal grill, but a curious creature from a galaxy far away.

"What could you possibly want with us?" I asked. The grill said with a high electric voice that his place back home was so clogged with roads and subdivisions and shopping malls that his people had sent him on a mission of discovery.

"Why, space visitor, do you look like a cooking instrument?" I asked.

He explained how his people had evolved into suburban appliances in order to save space. He wanted to know from us earthlings how we were dealing with excessive rates of growth.

I told him we didn't seem to be doing so great a job here where he had landed. I explained how we were in the middle, right this very moment, of trying to decide how much we would plan and how much we would let the forces of the market guide our growth.

"The market?" my visitor asked.

"You know, like gravity," I said. "It's something invisible but people trust it to decide almost everything."

"They trust it without seeing it?" he asked. "It must surprise them from time to time."

"Oh yes," I said. "All the time."

He was interested in how this so-called "market" had shaped Spartanburg County, so I loaded this grill-shaped alien up into my pickup truck, and I drove him out for an education in land-use planning. He listened as we drove around:

"Our county," I explained, "has had a sort of *de facto* zoning for decades."

"Oh, I see," he said. "This must be the 'I'm rich enough so I can buy a whole zip code and an asphalt plant will never move in next to me' zone."

"That's right, space visitor," I said. "Land use here has progressed entirely based on the desires of people."

"Interesting. What other zones have you developed through this flawed system, earthling?"

We drove around and I narrated: "Over here you've got the 'My treeless church parking lot is so big I could land the space shuttle there' zone. And that's the 'Can you believe how close I put my ugly concrete block business to the road?' zone."

He caught on fast and continued:

"And that must be the 'You will not believe the crap I've got piled and buried on my property' zone," our visitor said. "We have one like that on our planet."

"And here we have the 'This is how many single-wide trailers you can put in an old peach orchard' zone and the 'My empty big-box store will probably be empty for a decade because my lease is cheap' zone."

I took up where he left off:

"There's the 'Canopy trees? This is a shopping center parking lot, not a forest!' zone."

He answered with:

"Yes, earthling, and over there is the 'If they want to keep farming they ought to find a way to make a living doing it or sell that good flat land and let us put some patio homes there' zone."

Before we ran out of time I explained how I wanted to show him the "With a little imagination and a school board ready to deal, that high school's a Wal-Mart waiting to happen" zone, and the "Put this new school out here in this old cow pasture because I own it and we'll figure out later how to widen all the roads" zone.

"You Spartanburgers are a people of boundless imagination," the space visitor intoned from the pickup truck bed. "I can see we could drive forever through your past zoning experiments, but my fuel cell is low. I need to get home. Let us return to the wildflower landing pad."

So we drove back past one of my favorite failures of land use, the "Quick, clear-cut this river bottom before the tree-huggers come" zone, and turned into our suburban neighborhood.

"I wish you luck in working out your future," he said. "It sounds like your County Council has its work cut out for it," the alien said, and then his grill disappeared into the trees.

—April 20, 2007

Free-Range Stonescaper

We live in the Piedmont, a rocky area, and I'm a rock hound. I scan roadsides for rock piles on public right-of-ways. At 55 miles per hour I can judge the heft required to boost a boulder into the truck. If a rock is the right size to lift, I'll go back with my gloves and back brace and haul it to our yard.

The local rock merchants charge $130 per pallet. A free-ranging rock hound like me can surface-collect a pallet's worth of rocks on a trip up the Saluda Grade. Rock collecting is one of the main reasons I drive a pickup.

The local rock I find is not perfect, and the roadsides are no rock market. There's little choice as to color or size. You take whatever chance and luck give you. I think that's why I like it so much. The type of rock, gneiss, that's mostly in this area weathers quickly once it's on the surface and broken into pieces. It crumbles and crusts once it's exposed. It turns soft through the years. Moss grows easily on it. It makes whatever you might need for landscaping—walls, flowerbeds—but ultimately it also makes our soil.

I use our local rock to make flowerbeds mostly, but sometimes if one is long and slender I'll stand it on end in a shallow hole and pretend we live next to Stonehenge. I've even been known to invite friends over for a party on Summer Solstice and wait for the sun to set and then wander into the yard and stand a stone up at the precise spot the star disappears. Of course it's an imperfect practice based on line-of-sight judgments from our deck, not some Druid science passed down for a thousand years. If we live here for fifty years maybe I'll come closer to getting it right.

I'm no Druid, but having my hands on local rocks does make me feel intimate with this landscape in a way they would understand. Contact with rock is spiritual for me, a sacrament. I can see how rock made it into religion so often. It's as if I'm hefting the very bone of the land itself.

Buying rock (which I confess I have done to augment the local stone I find) makes me feel like I'm part of the free market, something that's never given me much spiritual pleasure. I'm sure Wal-Mart will someday soon find a way to sell landscaping stone by the pallet a few dollars cheaper than the local mom-and-pop rock shops. They'll mine it in China and haul it in freighters half-way around the world to make a profit. They'll make stone to use in your yard into a slick predictable commodity, but they'll never try and sell gneiss, our local stone. There's no profit to be found in such a sorry, mealy rock.

This past weekend I decided I needed another flowerbed along the driveway. I'd wedge it between the concrete and the oaks and give us a little summer color as we pulled in to park. I got my heavy-duty rock-moving wheelbarrow and headed onto the lot we own next door. I had a hunch there were rocks in the woods. Soon I hit the mother lode along a drainage right-of-way. There were manageable chunks of gneiss excavated decades ago when the drain pipe was buried.

One man's obstacle for digging is another man's treasure. I loaded the wheelbarrow and hauled three loads out of the woods.

Now my flowerbed is finished. I've got an odd-shaped space twenty-by-ten-feet filled with locally grown perennials, and I think they've got enough sun to keep blooming. I like the look of the irregular stone when I drive in. If I keep it moist through the summer I know moss will grow there. I like it that for millions of years this rock has been here, the bedrock for what one day would become a neighborhood. We've been here five years now. Looking at my flowers, it helps me remember the stone's got seniority over us and that will never change.

—May 25, 2007

River of Relations

Last Monday I drove with my friend Steve Patton thirty minutes up into North Carolina to the mill town of Cliffside. One of my eight great-grandparents, John Simeon Bradley, was born a couple of miles upstream near Henrietta, but what's more, it's where I've decided that I'll put in August 7th for my 200-mile mostly solo paddle to the sea.

The Second Broad River crosses Alternate 221 at Cliffside. The river there almost forms an oxbow and wiggles several more times before its confluence with the main branch of the Broad about two miles downstream. Finding a potential put-in for my trip was easy. There's a sewer pumping station just downstream with a path to the river. Others have used it. There are the remains of a campfire or two, and an old shopping cart stands marooned upstream on the rocks below the mill dam.

I like the symmetry of starting a long paddling adventure somewhere my long-ago progenitor also began a journey of discovery, a journey that really ended up here with me. John Bradley left Henrietta around 1900 to work the mills down here in Spartanburg.

My great-grandfather likely traveled the very same highway we took to check out my launch site. In Spartanburg John Bradley met my great-grandmother, a young woman named Ella Mabe, down from the hills of Virginia to work the mills as well. They married, and my grandmother Hulda Bradley was born in 1908. My mother, Mary Ellen, was born in 1926, and by that time we were only one small romantic collision away from 1954 and my birth. Relations are like a river, are always flowing downstream toward the clear waters of the present.

The mill at Cliffside is closed, as are all the mills my relatives worked in through three generations in Spartanburg, but Cone Mills still has an active textile business dyeing blue jeans in North Carolina. Right away we noticed that the color of the Second Broad is magenta. The water there at Cliffside looks like it's been stained with grape Kool-Aid. I made a joke with Steve about how I can tie an old pair of my jeans to the back of the kayak and darken them up a little in the waters of the Broad River. I'll be baptized in the industry that supported my mother's family for almost a hundred years.

I've been thinking about this 200-mile kayak trip since 2006 when I paddled to Columbia. This time I'll be alone most of the way. I'm planning to spend two weeks on the water. Friends and family will meet me several times for re-supply, but many days I'll have nothing to occupy the river miles but my own observations, the stories I can remember, and the songs I can hum.

Steve plans to meet me at the Lake Marion dam for the final fifty miles down the channel of the old Santee River. He's done the trip before, and he has familiar connections to the old Hampton Plantation where Archibald Rutledge lived. We're hoping to paddle from the Santee River channel up through old rice fields and visit the home—now an historic site—of the state's first and most famous poet laureate.

The paddling plan has a certain literary symmetry to it—from a blue river in North Carolina, downstream two weeks, to the land of the original South Carolina blue bloods. People have asked me if I'm concerned about mosquitoes and if I'm sure I'll have enough food. Where will I camp? Will I carry a cell phone? Will I fish?

I'll try to paddle fast enough to outrun the mosquitoes and have a good tent to keep them at bay at night. I will tuck a cell phone away in my pack and know from my trip to Columbia that service will be spotty at best. If Steve's right, then I'll meet anglers along the way who will give me fish, so I won't need to catch them myself. (The Broad is known for its bass, and I hope to fry a few over an open fire.) Whatever happens, I should get a good column or two out of it all. And when I get to the ocean I'll turn around and look back toward where I started, all the way back to Cliffside and John Simeon Bradley.

—July 13, 2007

River of the Carolinas

This week, drought and high August temperatures pushed my chance to paddle to the sea back into the planning stages. I'd planned to leave this week in my borrowed boat and arrive fourteen days later in the Santee delta.

But checking the Broad River gauge on the internet told me in no uncertain terms that the river's flow is down to one third of its usual level. The Weather Channel's ten-day forecast has the temperatures often well over 100 and the humidity not far behind. The paper says the "real feel" will be 112.

I want to write a book, so I've always imagined the story that will come out of my two-week trip to the ocean to be more float trip than ordeal.

Patience is one of the virtues being a fifty-something adventurer has taught me to work on, so instead of dropping my boat on the water, I read about someone else's river. I finally took down Henry Savage's *The Santee: River of the Carolinas* and consumed the book in a few air-conditioned sessions.

Henry Savage's book, released in 1956, is part of the famous "Rivers of America" series that published sixty-five volumes between 1937 and 1974. The popular series was conceived as a way to tell America about its history through river drainages. Written often by poets and novelists, "Rivers of America" proved enduring and instructive. Famous volumes include *Everglades, River of Grass* by Marjorie Stoneman Douglas and *The French Broad* by Wilma Dykeman. Andrew Wyeth's first book illustrations appeared in *The Brandywine*.

Though I have read several of the "Rivers of America" volumes, I was drawn to Savage's book because it is about where I live, my watershed, the river system that includes Lawson's Fork and the Pacolet. I was hopeful that by reading *The Santee* I would find a map for my own trip that I could update from 1956 until 2007. Surely Savage would stitch together the real-time natural history legacies of the Broad and the Saluda, the Catawba and the Wateree, the Congaree, and finally the Santee.

A few chapters into Savage's book I realized the river I was looking for would not be there. The Conway lawyer managed to write 400 fascinating pages and never approach the real river I was searching for. He sketched out bold, vivid scenes of South Carolina history—the plantation farmers, the frontier trappers, the canal builders, the war heroes like the Swamp Fox, and the politicians like John C. Calhoun—but the type of river lore I loved remained minimal. There was no first-person account of a single mile of the Santee River system. There was little talk of pollution or recovery of natural systems, no first-person prose rhapsody about a single specific spot on the river. After a brief chapter on the geography and geology of the river system Savage says, "… the story with which we are concerned, that of man and the river, has yet to begin."

How different we are, river writer Henry Savage and I. We are separated in time by half a century. Savage was given his voice by the period he wrote within. Did it ever occur to him to write a first-person narrative about his beloved Santee River system? Did it ever cross his mind to get a canoe, drive it to the headwaters of the Broad, the Catawba, or the Saluda and drop it in the water of a living, flowing stream? I'll never know the answers to these questions. I'll just let the river flow and take me where it will when I finally get on it.

Maybe I was looking for the wrong river when I opened up *The Santee*. Maybe Savage's mythic narrative about the human history that a watershed can hold is instructive for my twenty-first century nature writer's voice. "The river remembers!" he says in his last paragraph. "But life, like the river, flows on, and man, obsessed with immortality, looks forward into an uncertain future."

We are that future, and the river is still here. I'll paddle Savage's river and update it when the drought lifts. Maybe some day my book will take its place alongside his on a dusty library shelf to be picked up in fifty years by another generation's river voyager.

—August 10, 2007

In a Dry, Hot Season

Last week it was 100 degrees for four days in a row, the first time since the Upcountry started keeping records in 1918. One day about 4 p.m. the mercury officially topped out at 105. People were suffering in the abnormal heat, so we were among the lucky ones. Our air conditioning (thank goodness for human ingenuity) was humming along, but a few times a day I wandered outside into the world so I could feel it in my face, on my body—historic heat.

Each morning I took the dog down to the creek before the heat rose, but there wasn't much to see. The mighty Lawson's Fork was only a weak trickle. The old tire I use to gauge stream flow was all the way out of the water, something I haven't seen since we moved out here five years ago. It's been a full month with only a trace of rain, and the five months before that we had ten inches less than what we'd normally register. The only creatures enjoying this low water are the gray graceful herons observing the deep bends where the fish are congregating. The buffet's open all day, easy pickings for them.

The big, beautiful Piedmont hardwood trees started the year stressed from a late, hard frost. Now, dry and stressed again, they're dropping their leaves long before fall. The records will show it wasn't a very good year for photosynthesis. This year's growth ring will be thin.

In the floodplain understory the tender stemmed plants like jewelweed have shriveled and collapsed. There are fissures in the mud. The sand in the bends is dry as Arabia. If this pattern persists, and we keep getting thirty inches of rain per year instead of our normal forty-eight, then our woods could look like the Texas Hill Country outside of Austin. Can you say scrub oak and juniper?

I don't want to live in Texas. I like the rainforest feel of the humid South Carolina Piedmont woods. I'm at home if I'm surrounded by lush vegetation and full rivers. I want my winters cold and wet and my summers hot, but not too hot.

Human and Puny, that's what my friend Deno Trakas called a book of poems a few years ago. The title poem came from a dream he had in which a famous poet showed him to the back door. They'd been talking inside the poet's house about Deno's work, and the old poet had given him a bad review. Deno turns on the bottom step and says, "Well, that's because you're human, human and puny."

Of course what Deno means is that human beings—even great poets—are puny in the face of time. No matter what we achieve in life, human bodies age, and we slip away. To be human is to accept how frail we are in the end. One human cannot stand up to entropy, the great natural winding down of systems. At least that's how I read his poem.

But there's another way to look at it all: to be human is also to possess the power to cause great change over time, for better or for worse. Since the Industrial Revolution our species has brought about the complete alteration of our planet—from your backyard to the Arctic, there is not a square mile of land or ocean that has not been changed by our presence. We humans invented air conditioning, but we also put a hole in the ozone. We've built malls and fast-food strips for convenience and profit, but we're responsible for mass extinctions and unprecedented habitat destruction. We drive fast and our windows are electric, but we're melting the glaciers. We have tinkered our way into a position where it looks like we have altered the very weather itself.

So individually we're human and puny, but collectively we've changed everything we've touched, even on a planetary level. Remember this last week of 100-degree days. You sweated through an historic moment. You might have even seen the future, and it's too hot.

—August 17, 2007

Summer River Scout Trip

The heat and drought did in my epic summer paddle to the sea, and I decided to put it off until next May. In spite of low water and 100-degree days I was able to get in three river trips and an overnight before school started.

On the first day out of town Steve Patton and I paddled through Columbia on the Broad and Congaree rivers. The water was low, but I wanted to check out that shallow, rocky passage of the Broad I'd always crossed on I-126 coming into the capital city.

The old saying goes that in the summer the only thing between Hades and Columbia is a screen door. There are also several rivers. Though there were a million Carolinians sweltering in the heat in all directions, I admired how two fishermen beached their aluminum canoe in the shallows and sat belly-deep in fold-out chairs, cooling off.

When we reached the confluence of the Broad with the Saluda the water of the Congaree proved icy cold. College students in inner tubes bobbed past, pulling sidecars with coolers. The river looked like a watery city park. We'd forgotten the Saluda River is released off the bottom of the Lake Murray Dam and so the midland current is cold enough for mountain trout. We took one more dip to cool down before exiting at the Gervais Street Bridge in the mid-day

Columbia heat.

The next day we drove upstream on the Broad River above Gaffney to an area called Ninety-Nine Islands. Here there are two old dams, and I wanted to scout passages around each. I'd rest easier until next May if I knew how I could get me, my boat, and my gear around these concrete river plugs.

Access was easy. We found a boat landing on the map above Ninety-Nine Island Dam, parked the truck, and paddled along the shore of the long, narrow Upcountry lake. A little sign across from the landing told us that the portage route below was on river left, so I felt better knowing where to exit the river. This Ninety-Nine Island Dam can be dangerous. Once, the guidebooks tell you, a fisherman was swept over the seventy-one-foot dam to his death, but the portage route is safely upstream.

After an hour of paddling we'd finally outrun the impoundment. A half-mile below Cherokee Falls Dam, the river current returns, and the slack water disappears. With a little zig-zagging behind rocks we pulled up behind the low dam and powerhouse built right on top of a long shoals. The portage at Cherokee Falls is on river right. Along the way we saw ospreys, wood ducks, and egrets. The birds don't seem to mind the heat.

Our third scouting trip was down to the lower Santee below Lake Marion, the stretch of the river above McClellanville called "the French Santee" because it was settled in the eighteenth century by French Huguenots with names like Huger, Gervais, Poinsett, and Mannigault.

We arrived late in the day and camped deep in Francis Marion National Forest, surrounded by live oaks, slash and loblolly pines. We were the only ones in the wilderness campsite save two men Steve called "national forest gypsies," who'd been camping there for weeks, foraging in the forest for edible mushrooms. A smoky campfire kept the mosquitoes at bay, and at dusk a great horned owl hunted around the edges of the campground.

The next morning, we paddled several miles from a Forest

Service boat landing down Wambaw Creek to the South Santee. On the way out five or six small alligators slipped down pluff-mud banks into the water as we passed. Night herons roosted in the cypress. By the time we reached the river I felt we were alone with the current and the sky. Once rice fields as far as you could see, the lower Santee is now a ragged, linear wilderness.

On the way back we had a little unexpected river adventure. We paddled up on the king of alligators in the middle of the creek. Its head was wide as two canoe paddles, and by the distance between snorkeling snout and eyes what we couldn't see looked to be close to ten feet long. When the regal reptile finally decided to submerge, the surging wake bounced our canoe like a whitewater flume. I've seen plenty of alligators but I'm always surprised how impressive a big one can be, and even my heart fluttered a little.

Adventure over, we drove back to Spartanburg, the school year approaching like a flood. It takes about four hours to drive from the Upcountry to the lower Santee. By canoe it's two weeks. Out on the water you can forget the heat, and even in this historic drought there's enough water to float on most rivers. It's good to remember that from the Upcountry, it's all downstream.

—August 31, 2007

Whose Planet Is It Anyway?

It's easy to draw negative conclusions about yellow jackets. They seem to us humans to always be in bad moods, and so they are hard to love. They have little charisma. Though yellow jackets make good football mascots, they would not be on anyone's short list for the next pilot cuddly creature show on Animal Planet.

Yellow jackets seem ill-tempered and scary. We associate them with picnics gone wrong. These small wasps can even be deadly if they come swarming unexpectedly out of an unseen nest and you, dear reader, happen to be allergic to their stings. I'm not allergic, but I've had three memorable encounters with yellow jackets in my life—once in my teens and twice in adulthood. All three times I was cutting grass and I disturbed a ground nest, and the next thing I knew I was doing a frightful dance, swatting a swarm of little buzz saws.

This time of year they seem particularly ornery. Maybe it's because a colony of yellow jackets expands in the late summer and early fall, the workers looking for food. After all, they'll all be dead come winter except the yellow jacket queen. She'll survive and next spring nest, lay eggs, and build her wasp queendom anew.

I lay all this out in order to get to the yellow jacket nest on the trail behind our house and the eco-ethical dilemma it presents me every day. For three weeks I've known the nest was there and have watched it on my walks. The entrance to the nest is a marvel of insect construction, a perfect one-inch hole in the dry Piedmont mud worn smooth by thousands of take-offs and landings. The yellow and black wasps come and go at a rate of three to five at a time. I stroll close enough to see all this, then take a wide berth to pass it by.

The nest is not on the trail but slightly off to the side. When I first saw it my impulse was to run back up the hill, as most of my friends would do, fill a soft drink bottle with gasoline and finish it off, a first strike that would secure the trail for my daily walk. So what's the ethical dilemma of bringing a little shock and awe to a bunch of wasps? Why not wipe the colony out?

Well, first of all, yellow jackets are native wasps. To be native is something I respect and admire and try to preserve. That alone in my hierarchy of plants and animals gives yellow jackets status over even the more even-tempered honey bees, their imported non-native cousins we've been clever enough to adapt to our own uses. As natives of this place, yellow jackets deserve to do the work they evolved for—pollination and procreation.

Next, these deep-in-the-woods trailside yellow jackets are wild. They don't need me any more than I want them. Their ancestors built nests in the ground like this for millions of years, and their wild ways haven't been altered much in 20,000 years of humans like me walking around them.

Because of how they have evolved, yellow jackets are interesting models as social animals go. Their community rules are clear. They nest. They secure food and water. Some of them mate with the queen. They protect their colony if it seems threatened, say by a lawn mower, or a careless walker who steps on their entry hole.

Every day I stand and ponder this nest and the slate of decisions it presents. Live and let live, or take it out because it might be a threat? Shape a life-lesson out of my reaction to this colony of bad-tempered wasps? See it for what it is—a "Kudzu" column just waiting to be written?

Out of my observations I've concluded that it's their planet as much as it is mine, and I'll let this colony of wasps live out the seasonal cycle that will do them in anyway when the frost comes. My action will leave one more queen ready to start again in the spring, one more little dot on the wild map of the Upstate.

—September 7, 2007

In Dreams Begin Reality

I've been thinking a great deal this week about vision—how it happens, how it affects community, how it morphs (and sometimes transmogrifies) from wild, bold ideas into something people can work inside and celebrate.

It takes time and resources and luck for a big idea to get from a human brain (or a committee of brains) to bricks and mortar. In the beginning maybe one person has an idea, or there are rounds of visioning sessions, *charrettes*. Masterplans are passed and saluted. Resources either fall into place or they do not.

Most often the original idea and the final product don't match up. Almost always there is a diminishment of that initial bold vision as we design, gather resources, and finally break ground (a complex and exciting metaphor).

With diminishment of vision often comes a sort of satisfaction. Things get done. We build, frame, top out the superstructure. No matter what the initial vision, we almost always feel pride in any project completed. It's human nature. We point to a building or an organization and say, "Once this was only air, an idea."

Is it enough? Is something, as a friend of mine likes to say, always better than nothing? This is a hard question for a community to answer, and the answer is often on the move. It takes time and energy and resources for a city to decide. Community dreams are interlocking and layered. Some people (and they are often the people with the original vision still in their heads) find it hard to be satisfied with reality. For other people reality is comforting and solid. It's worth the price of admission, no matter what the compromises to the original vision.

What has brought on my musings about vision is three recent events: the important opening of the Chapman Cultural Center on five acres of the Renaissance tract on Saint John Street, the announcement of USC-Upstate's plan to build a downtown business school, and a mail-out rendering of what the rest of the nineteen-acre, city-owned, undeveloped Renaissance tract could look like if planned around a series of lakes and waterfalls cascading down the hill to Daniel Morgan Avenue.

The first event, the opening of the Chapman Cultural Center, is a well-documented and celebrated vision-made-reality, and I won't dwell on it here. Let me just say that with the opening of our cultural campus on Saint John Street we now have our Peace Center, though much more modest in scale than its Greenville counterpart. This cultural center will serve our community well. The Chapman Center's two matching buildings, its plaza, and Greek-style temple theater give the beaux arts and culture of this city an important central presence like no other since the Opera House came down in 1906.

The second event, the announcement of the business school, is exciting and visionary as well. Greenville lost its major downtown college in the 1950s when Furman moved ten miles out into the suburbs. Wofford and Converse have remained and flourished on their original downtown Spartanburg campuses. With the move of the USC-Upstate business school onto the Renaissance site the city takes another step toward truly becoming a college town.

And then there's the third thing, that unexpected spiral-bound proposal with the logo of a local real estate company on the cover letter that's now making the rounds of this community. It renders a central city Renaissance village centered on water. It makes interesting and evocative claims for this dramatic Renaissance site.

Is this dream practical? Are there public-private resources for such a vision? Those might be the wrong questions to ask for now. We can never have enough vision at the beginning of things, and for our community's resurgence, we're still near dawn.

It's entirely possible somebody might decide to make it happen, or some version of it nipped and tucked by the constraints of reality. Vision's a funny thing. It's hard to keep in a can. It's like lightning, and it strikes or it doesn't.

But who knows? It seems no coincidence that this proposal was mailed out just prior to the opening of the Chapman Center. Those who prepared this vision built around water are hopeful Spartanburg's community leaders will gather at the center on the hill this week, gaze off to the north, and think, "Well, what if we did have a series of ponds and waterfalls down there?"

—October 5, 2007

Abiding Images

It's seven in the morning. Coffee steams from my cup and I've been up for nearly an hour. I've already been out with the dog. It's cool today, a good break from all the unseasonably warm weather we've had. The drought has lifted for a little while. My rain gauge, unemptied, still tells me that we had over an inch and a half of rain last week here east of Spartanburg. It's felt like the South again for a few days—moist and verdant. Now autumn has suddenly arrived, and the dry weather will likely return if the patterns hold true. The sourwood trees are turning that burnt red that for me signals fall. Winter is only twelve weeks away.

People often ask me how I write these columns. They seem genuinely interested in my creative process. Well, this sitting at the desk is the most of it—discipline and repetition are the most common elements on the periodic table of creativity. If it's Monday morning, I know where I'll be, sitting here in my study, tapping a keyboard. For over two years I've risen on Mondays, sat down, faced the computer screen, and shaped a 700-word column out of something I've heard or thought or imagined. I've written about what makes me mad, and what makes me laugh, or what I don't seem to understand, or what I can't ignore. This column happens to be number 123.

Discipline doesn't explain where the columns come from, though. It only explains how they get typed out. They come from attention, a skill I've tried to practice for most of my adult life. Natural history taught me this skill. I might forget to take out the garbage, but I look and listen and smell for the details that will end up on a page every Monday morning. I follow my attention to the edges of my environment. This is something I learned from my field scientist friends. When I've tagged along with field scientists they always have been tuned into signs of the life around them. They see things first, and they see what they see in relation to all that has come before. This is good training for a writer and great training for a columnist.

I started out my writing life thirty years ago as a poet, and being a columnist is more like writing a poem than you might believe. A draft of a poem is usually short, something you can do in one sitting, and it's often focused on a picture in your mind, or something you've heard, or a sensation, what my poet friend Cathy Smith Bowers calls "an abiding image." By an abiding image Cathy means a haunting, something you can't seem to let go, that returns no matter what you do with your day-to-day life to forget it. The image abides, and as a poet you work with it until you have a draft of a poem.

As for me, sometimes on these Monday mornings I've got notes scrawled on the back of a used envelope, and other times I have an issue in my mind—landfills, clear cuts, four-wheelers, migrating butterflies, community vision.

So, all that said, there's a single abiding image, a story actually, that has seized me this morning. It's a white-tailed deer story we heard while out walking the dog in our neighborhood yesterday:

One of our neighbors was out blowing leaves. We stopped to chat and somehow the subject of deer came up. Our neighbor has a fenced backyard and two boxers. One day last week he was looking out the window and a deer had paused at the back fence, staring at the dogs. The boxers were barking, but the deer wasn't spooked. It began to run up and down the fence line, the dogs running with it, back and forth. Our neighbor called his wife, but by the time she got to the window the deer had bolted at a full run.

A few minutes later the dogs were barking again. Our neighbor looked out, and the frisky deer was back, running the fence, then took off to circle through the neighborhood at a full run. "To make a long story short, the deer returned five times," my neighbor said, smiling, the leaf blower hanging at his side.

—October 12, 2007

A Place Apart

One percent of the land in the lower forty-eight states is what might be considered wilderness.

Ninety-nine percent is utilized in some way for human profit—urban areas, suburbs, logging, mining, grazing. In 10,000 short years we humans have found ways to extend our shadow over the whole reach of a peopleless continent.

During the first 9,500 years Native American economies created the changes—mostly through hunting pressure and agriculture. Once European settlement began, things speeded up, as Jared Diamond likes to say, through the use of "guns, germs, and steel."

We can look at this settlement and utilization of the continent as a supreme accomplishment, or we can ask, "What happened? Why did humans get out of control?" We can see space as something humans were given dominion over by God, or we can see an unhealthy range extension, the way an animal might extend its territory when the opportunity arises.

Both positions have been researched and studied. Both have support in books and ideologies. Most people probably fall somewhere between the extremes.

The idea of utility came up in my class as well this week. Students finished up a project on small, isolated wetlands and all the issues revolving around their preservation in South Carolina.

After doing a good deal of reading, writing a paper, and engaging in spirited discussion, there seemed to be two positions among the young scholar/citizens: protect isolated wetlands entirely, no matter what, or protect them up to a point. That point for these students seemed to be utilitarian: "What's in it for us humans?"

Both positions seemed reasonable, though they are complicated because they need to be carried out by law, and law in South Carolina favors utility. It favors the idea of land as property. It almost always privileges use over pure protection, and any time the scale starts tilting the other way, someone will come along and remind us of that legal privilege.

Last week there was an article in a local paper about a lawmaker complaining that the 33,000 acres of state land in the Jocassee Gorges in Oconee and Pickens counties isn't well utilized.

The state acquired the wild reach of property a decade ago, and Larry Martin, a Republican senator from Pickens, believes there hasn't been enough human traffic for our public investment. We should advertise the fifty-two square miles of wild state land, improve the roads, mark the trails better.

Utility or preservation? As usual, when issues like this come up, my mind wanders back to my own past experience.

In 1980 I lived on Cumberland Island, a National Seashore off the coast of Georgia. I worked at Greyfield Inn, one of the few private inholdings on the island. Visitation to Cumberland was limited to boat traffic, most coming from the park service ferry that left once a day from the mainland dock. Some in Congress wanted to build a bridge and make the island just like many of the other nearby sea islands. They wanted public access, twenty-four hours a day.

Others wanted to preserve what they thought was a "wild and endangered" experience: a trip by boat to a place apart. The preservationists won that battle. There's still no bridge to Cumberland.

Two years earlier I'd worked for a poet in Port Townsend,

Washington. He had bought ten acres of cut-over cedar and manzanita woodland on a bluff overlooking Discovery Bay. He'd built a small house by hand for his family on the property, which had been "well-utilized" by a logging company and then sold off for house sites.

My poet-boss had set aside two of his ten acres as a sort of personal preserve, a place he would never enter as long as he owned the land. It was a sort of an ecological thought experiment.

Why didn't he go there? Why did the trail he cut to the bluffs skirt clear of those two acres? He wanted a spot on his property that he could say he didn't need. He wanted to know that, at least for him, there was a spot nearby that was philosophically free from conventional utility.

It may sound silly now, but this thought experiment made a tremendous impact on the mind of a twenty-something like me, still forming my opinions about land use.

Why shouldn't there be places outside the reach of utility? Why can't we simply leave a few places free from our utilitarian logic? I'm still weighing the answers.

—November 23, 2007

Where the Wild Things Are

Our house is turned to the linear wildness along the creek like a big ear.

We listen for what happens in the timber and thick undergrowth below us with the fascination of someone sampling a new CD.

If I hear a bird I don't know, I try to track it down for identification, adding its name to our "play list" of what this place might spin in our direction. I scribble the name in the back of an old field guide, a note as to what is passing by.

The narrow finger of woods behind our house is part of an interstate highway system for wildlife, a corridor running along the Broad, Pacolet, and Lawson's Fork, broken only in places where human habitation has pinched it shut or roads cross it and turn it into a killing zone.

It runs from the ocean all the way to our backyard. Beyond us this corridor continues all the way to Inman. Most people don't see the land this way, as a watery set of fingers reaching upstream and down.

Hunters think this way, but most people don't think like a moving animal. Instead, people of the suburbs and cities focus on roads and airways and where those may take us.

I'm not saying wild birds and animals don't go overland, from ridge to ridge. They do. They also migrate along the waterways in great numbers.

On Halloween night we heard a new song in the woods down by the creek.

"Listen," Betsy said. "It sounds like mad dogs from Hades."

With all our listening we were used to the sound of wild dogs chasing deer, or feral cats mating in the bottomland. This was different. It was a new set of chords the night had plucked.

Three or four more nights in November we woke up to the musical yips and gurgles in the middle of the night. It was a chorus of foreign sounds moving up and down the creek.

It didn't sound like any canine I knew, but I had my suspicions. Walking Toby early in the morning I'd see fresh scat on the trail that looked very dog-like, only this had shiny persimmon seeds in it.

"Coyotes," I finally speculated. "It has to be coyotes on the creek."

Then, the night before Thanksgiving, we finally heard them howl. The disordered yipping finally broke into two distinct howls like we all used to hear on Western movies, Wile E. Coyote howls, long and lonely with a hint of desert music in them.

Every night since has been full of anticipation. If we hear them, we wake and crank the windows open.

There are logical human arguments against coyotes in our neighborhood. They harass what little livestock remains, raid turkey nests, chase deer, carry rabies, and kill pets.

They're not native to the Southeast and have only moved in because they are relentless breeders and opportunists. They exploit the marginal pastureland and settled suburbs. It's perfect habitat.

I know all this, but I still love the coyotes howling and listen every night to hear them again. They remind me of my travel out West. They add mystery to my place. Scholars talk about iconographic images like the American flag-raising on Iwo Jima or John Kennedy waving to the crowd from an open-topped car in Dallas.

There are sounds in nature that take on the status of icons as well. A hawk's whistle or a howl in the woods announces wildness, otherness, distance from what it is to be human.

We used to have gray wolves and red wolves here. They used to call this creek home. We wiped them out, and they're probably not coming back.

Now mostly we have beagles and German longhaired dachshunds roaming among us. But the nightly howls remind me that wildness is also on the run behind our house. Whatever reminds me of its eternal and essential presence is worth a listen.

—November 30, 2007

Unpaving Paradise

We live on a cul-de-sac. That's a fancy French way of saying we live on a short, lollipop-shaped, dead-end, asphalt turn-around in the suburbs.

The cul-de-sac is one of the basic units of twentieth century subdivisions, brought to us by the designers of sprawl. Cul-de-sacs are often the termination point of an outmoded settlement system that includes larger collector roads and distant shopping centers.

Our cul-de-sac is a broad oval of black petroleum pavement and has served well as a basketball court and overflow parking for parties. It's big enough for a large truck to turn around in without shifting into reverse, but it's also small enough that I can imagine it not there.

When this subdivision was laid out in the 1980s, the real estate plan called for three lots on our street, each approaching an acre. People back then didn't think much about carbon footprints or sprawl. Pavement was a good thing, and cul-de-sacs were part of the prosperity plan. Pavement signified progress. Dusty dirt roads were the past, some frontier relic. Gravel was an undergarment. The future was paved with asphalt.

When we were looking for a lot in 2001 we were drawn to this street because it still had these three vacant lots that almost backed up to the creek. There was the illusion of country. There was a sense that you were living on the edge of the city.

That was five years ago, and since we moved in all the lots in the little subdivision have sold, and there are plans in the works to build on all of them. Sensing the demographic pressure, we scrambled to buy the lots on either side, securing our treescape, controlling the asphalt circle in front of our house. We justified our action by calling the purchases "investments."

But now I'm thinking that our cul-de-sac's useful life might be over. I'm thinking more and more about removing it, getting the county to close the street, and converting it into a narrow driveway.

I've come to think more about impervious surfaces like our cul-de-sac since the drought, and I'm seeing run-off surfaces everywhere. I've become acutely aware of all those extra parking spaces at the mall that are only used on the Friday after Thanksgiving. I'm watching our stream dry up not only because we're getting less rain, but because of a drop in groundwater. I'm noticing that the creek behind our house runs higher and quicker when it rains. Normal flow is less, and flood flow flashes down the channel, eroding the banks.

Now that we own the whole cul-de-sac, I dream daily of dismantling it, reducing what I've come to call our "asphalt footprint." Every day when I come home I scheme about how I'd like to leave the planet with a little less pavement and add a little more pervious surface. Our individual action could add a little more groundwater to recharge the creek.

But there are so many details to consider in this experiment in dismantling a little paved stretch of the American dream—for instance, how to restore the contours of the original land that a bulldozer once reduced to grade for a street. Our lot slopes to the creek, and the highest point of the ridge is along the feeder street coming in. Will I have to bring in tons of fill dirt? How much will that cost? How many hours of bulldozer time will I have to buy (add that to our carbon footprint!) in order to restore this circle of suburban land to what it was before our cul-de-sac existed?

What will I do with the asphalt once I tear it up? Cut it up in squares and build a retaining wall? Dig a hole and bury it? Would that pollute the groundwater? And what about all those concrete curb slabs? What to do with them?

Maybe I simply need to learn to live with the mistakes of the past. Maybe I should just accept our cul-de-sac and imagine that sometime in the future when we're long gone, someone might want two more houses side by side with this one.

Or, maybe not. Someday maybe I'll figure out all the details and launch into my own little restoration project for a few hundred square feet of Piedmont forest right here in "Suburban Nation."

—December 7, 2007

A Whole Lot of Shaking
Going on

We had a little earthquake last week. Its 6 a.m. epicenter was near the town of Columbus, North Carolina. It wasn't much, just a 3.1 magnitude shaking for a few seconds, but the local paper reported it was enough to make some poor child up there wake up thinking that his brimstone preacher was right and the end of time had arrived on schedule.

It touched me to hear about that little boy's fear of time ending, but I wanted to drive up there and do a little mission work, preach a little geology at him. I wanted to make sure he was as versed in the great story of the earth as he was in biblical apocalypse.

Earthquakes, even more than the poor, will be with us always, and rather than signs of the end of time, they witness to time's vast sweep. They are part of what geologists call "the big picture," a narrative of billions of years of deep time that guides science's understanding of the planet's localized burps and gurgles.

As the geologists have come to understand it, the movement of the earth originates from faults, either shallow or deep, in the crust. When two faulted blocks of rock slip a little, we feel it on the surface as a quake. As the Upcountry found out once again last week, Alaska and California aren't the only places where quakes can shake us awake. The whole continent is faulted. Some places—like our

West Coast—have more active faults because they are at the edges of two huge continental plates that are currently slamming against each other. One plate collides with the other, and they thrust above or plunge below the huge plate of rock next door. This collision zone is so active that earthquakes happen on a daily basis. "The big one" is what everyone's waiting for in California, and when it happens it will feel for a moment like the Second Coming.

But when the smoke clears and the damage is assessed, even that huge West Coast natural disaster will be seen as what it is—another small brush stroke in "the big picture" that geologists have painted for the whole planet.

We live on the calmer side of the continent. Our super-active earthquake time was hundreds of millions of years in the past. That's when the plate Africa is riding on was grinding against our east coast. Now Africa is in reverse, and the Atlantic Ocean has filled the great rift between the two plates. Things in our neighborhood have settled down, but not entirely. There are still old faults deep in the earth, and they still move.

On the evening of August 31, 1886, the city of Charleston experienced the most destructive earthquake ever recorded east of the Mississippi. It was not quite as intense as the 1811 New Madrid, Missouri, earthquake that made the Mississippi reverse its course in a move even Moses would envy, or the 1906 San Francisco quake, but the evidence tells us it was big: an estimated 7.6 on the not-yet-invented Richter Scale.

The quake was miles deep in the earth, and the rock on each side of the fault was displaced almost six feet. The sediments of the coastal plain where Charleston is built turned to mush over the quake area and rolled like waves on the sea.

The earthquake's results were catastrophic: 14,000 brick chimneys collapsed, ninety percent of the brick buildings in Charleston were damaged, and 110 people were killed. There was damage in all the large towns within a hundred miles of Charleston. In Columbia people reported difficulty walking during the quake.

If you visit Charleston on a regular basis you should not worry too much about the next "big one" there. In "the big picture" the odds are pretty small you'll experience it. Geologists have calculated that the 1886 earthquake was a one in 1,000 year event. That doesn't mean another big one can't happen tomorrow; just don't bet on it.

And what of the "end of time" that little boy in Columbus is worried about? I don't think anyone has successfully calculated the odds on that. Like many of the human hopes and fears in our day-to-day lives, that's a matter of faith, not science.

—December 14, 2007

Why Write about Nature?

This past weekend I drove to Charlottesville, Virginia, to speak at a reading sponsored by the Southern Environmental Law Center (SELC), a group responsible for some of the best and most important conservation work being done in the South. I like to think of the SELC as the legal voice for Southern land and animals.

They had my friend Janisse Ray and me up in celebration of their Philip Reed Award, which we both have won in the past. They asked us to talk about nature writing, to speak to why we write about nature.

I told the audience how for me, the question is not why I write about nature, but why I write mostly about this piece of the natural world, the Piedmont of the Carolinas. I explained how one particular assignment had shifted my literary attention.

In 1999 I received the dream call for a nature writer. An editor at National Geographic Books was on the line and said they were working on a big picture book called *Heart of a Nation*. I'd been recommended as one of the twelve essayists to write about some place dear to my own nature writer's heart. The editor offered a hefty fee and said I could write about any place I loved in the country. They sweetened the pot by saying they'd pay my way to spend some time in the place I selected. Of course I said yes then and there, and after that was settled, the editor gave me a week to make up my mind on what piece of the American landscape I would write about.

Anywhere in America! Where would I go? What would I say? I loved Wyoming's Big Horns and Washington State's Olympic Mountains out west. I knew the Everglades intimately and had lived on Georgia's Cumberland Island National Seashore. Maybe I could use National Geographic's dime and revisit them. Then it hit me: Why not write about my own neighborhood, a river called the Pacolet, the watershed my drinking water was drawn from, the place where my uncle had worked in cotton mills, and though I had been a kayaker for twenty years, a stream I'd never dropped a boat in?

"The Pacolet River?" the editor asked when I called a week later to accept the offer and report my essay topic. "Where the heck is the Pacolet River?"

To their credit the editors encouraged me and helped me shape what was at that time one of the first essays I'd written about my home ground. "From the Pacific coast to the Brooks Range, from Yosemite to the Pacolet," announced the advertising packet for *Heart of a Nation* sent to tens of thousands of potential buyers a year later.

So the folks in Charlottesville got to hear how as a Southern nature writer I'm now most interested in speaking for the places that have become sanctuary through neglect, abandonment, or abuse. In other words, as a writer I'm interested in the Old South made New South—abandoned rice fields, old canals, Piedmont quarries, collapsed mountain house sites deep in recovering forest, Girl Scout camps once set aside for recreation, local rivers like the Pacolet many think too fouled (or mundane) to celebrate or even to paddle.

What engages my imagination in these places is that somehow scraps of Southern wildness—a salt marsh on Ossabaw Island, a mountain cove in the Smokies, or Forty Rock Heritage Preserve in the Upcountry of South Carolina—have survived 200 years of farming, industrial logging, and the building of our cities and the suburbs. They still can engage my imagination as clearly as Ansel Adams' Half Dome or Thoreau's Maine Woods or Terry Tempest Williams' canyon lands.

I walk into these true preserves and I encounter plants and creatures there that don't seem affected by the I-85 corridor sprawl closing in around them. There are still rare stands of big trees, tiny wild gingers like the dwarf-flowered heartleaf found only in two Upcountry counties. There are muskrats, black rat snakes, anoles, slimy salamanders, leopard frogs, and Fowler's toads living their lives untroubled (or so it seems on the surface) by the sprawl and spread of our suburban and urban comfort zones.

Before I started writing about the ground under my feet, I used to think I needed the deep wildness of the far West for fulfillment. I still travel, but now I go to those powerful places as a brief visitor, not so much as a pilgrim. The South is my home ground. I write about what I know—but I also know how little remains of the glory that once was.

—March 30, 2007

About the Author

"Kudzu Telegraph" columns are only one aspect of John Lane's varied career as a writer, teacher, and advocate for sustainable growth, community, and wildness. He has published eleven other books of poetry and prose, most recently *Circling Home* (2007). One of his essays on Camp Mary Elizabeth was named a winner of the Phillip D. Reed Memorial Award for Outstanding Writing on the Southern Environment from the Southern Environmental Law Center. For over twenty years he has taught literature and writing at Wofford College, and in 2008 he was named the director of the college's new Glendale Shoals Environmental Studies Center, where he will teach environmental studies on the banks of his beloved Lawson's Fork. For more information about John's work and life check regularly at www.kudzutelegraph.com.

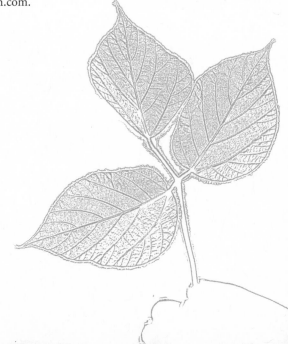

Acknowledgements

Since the first appearance of the digital Kudzu Telegraph in 1999 I've had the people of the Upcountry to thank. They've kept reading my opinions, first online and then for the last three years, week after week in the Community Journals.

A writer needs an audience to keep going. Because of the strong readership of the Community Journals there's never been any doubt about someone out there to read my column—either friend or stranger. After the columns are out in the world readers email me. They stop me in the aisles of the grocery store. They even write real letters with stamps on them about individual columns.

Particularly I'd like to thank Lyn Riddle, Gary Henderson, and the management of the Community Journals for opening up space every week for "Kudzu Telegraph."

As always I'd like to thank Betsy. She reads the columns first after I write them, and before you do.

The Hub City Writers Project is a non-profit organization whose mission is to foster a sense of community through the literary arts. We do this by publishing books from and about our community; encouraging, mentoring, and advancing the careers of local writers; and seeking to make Spartanburg a center for the literary arts.

Our metaphor of organization purposely looks backward to the nineteenth century when Spartanburg was known as the "hub city," a place where railroads converged and departed.

At the beginning of the twenty-first century, Spartanburg has become a literary hub of South Carolina with an active and nationally celebrated core group of poets, fiction writers, and essayists. We celebrate these writers—and the ones not yet discovered—as one of our community's greatest assets. William R. Ferris, former director of the Center for the Study of Southern Cultures, says of the emerging South, "Our culture is our greatest resource. We can shape an economic base … And it won't be an investment that will disappear."